The Complete
ASIAN
HEALTH & DIET
Cookbook

Mary Trevelyan Hodder

HEIAN

For Peter
who helped in every phase —
from prep and cooking to eating and cleanup

The Complete Asian Health & Diet Cookbook
by Mary Trevelyan Hodder

Photographs by Goh Sai Hock of 3rd Eye Photography

Illustrations by Stephanie Ryland

Cooking for photography by Mrs. Devagi Shanmugan

Props for photography lent by Tangs, except for Thai crockery courtesy of
Chao Phaya Thai Seafood Market and Restaurant

© Times Book International, Singapore

FIRST AMERICAN EDITION 1988

HEIAN INTERNATIONAL, INC.
P.O. BOX 1013
UNION CITY, CA 94587 USA

ISBN: 0-89346-302-7

Printed in Singapore

Contents

Rice, Noodles, Pastas, Breads and Cereals — 89

Soups, Stews and Salads — 121

Preface

Since 1982, when I began work on *The Complete Asian Health and Diet Plan,* there has been an explosion in health and diet awareness among the Asian public. The average person — educated by public and private health practitioners, books, local and international press and the broadcast media — knows more than ever about health matters, and is beginning to take an active role in managing his or her own health, diet and fitness programmes.

The Complete Asian Health and Diet Plan was the first health and fitness book written specifically for lovers of Asian food. It outlines the principles of good nutrition, stressing a varied and balanced Asian diet that, combined with a reasonable exercise programme, promotes improved health and safe weight loss without dieting.

The Complete Asian Health and Diet Cookbook follows the nutritional guidelines outlined in my first book and applies them to favourite Asian and international recipes, making them lower in fat and kilocalories, and retaining as much of their good taste as possible. This book gives yet another tool for vital, healthy living.

Acknowledgements

I would like to thank Anna Jacob Chacko (M.Sc. Food Service Management and Dietetics) for her assistance in preparing the nutritional information accompanying each recipe. I owe appreciation to Madam Choi Young Suck for contributing the Korean recipes. Special thanks also go to my editor, Jane Kohen Winter, for her dedication to this project. Thanks are also due to: Miss Tan Lui of Tangs for her valuable help in selecting the props for photography; the management of Chao Phaya Thai Seafood Market and Restaurant for lending the crockery for the photograph of Thai food; Mrs. Devagi Shanmugam for her superb organisation of the cooking for photography; Bavani Gunasekaran for her assistance in the kitchen; Goh Sai Hock of 3rd Eye Photography for his creative expertise; Mr. C. B. Tan of Sia Huat Pte. Ltd. for allowing us to purchase only a small quantity of milkshake glasses for photography; and Stephanie Ryland for prompt delivery of her elegant illustrations.

There are plenty of cookbooks available that cater to special diets — low-sodium, low-fat, low-calorie, vegetarian, the list goes on. Many of them are excellent, but they all involve the concept of a special diet, and almost all are based on Western foods and Western cuisine. None, however, has been written for the average Asian reader who likes to eat and who simply wants to improve his or her health — without sacrificing the pleasures of superb Asian cuisine.

This book aims to strike a reasonable balance between traditional Asian recipes and the nutritional guidelines for improved health outlined in my previous book. In developing the recipes, I have emphasised good taste as much as good health — because no matter how healthy a dish is, if it doesn't look and taste good, people won't eat it.

In *The Complete Asian Health and Diet Cookbook* I've updated favourite Asian recipes — made them healthier and more wholesome based on what we know about good nutrition and its role in lifelong health. There's a wide variety of delicious, full-flavoured dishes to choose from — Chinese, Malay, Indian, Nonya, Indonesian, Japanese, Vietnamese, Korean, Thai and a good selection of international dishes commonly eaten in Asia. The changes are all moderate, and easy to live with, and, for the most part, the dishes are relatively easy to prepare.

As you know, only gradual, moderate, easy to live with improvements in diet are likely to be permanent improvements. The recipes and tips for healthy cooking in this book can help you improve your diet slowly, painlessly and permanently. In a short time, you will be used to (and enjoying) healthy cooking and eating. You will improve your chances for a long and healthy life and, if you need to reduce body fat, you will lose weight naturally and effortlessly. I wish you enjoyable, healthy cooking and eating!

Introduction

About the Recipes

The recipes in this book are naturally low or reduced in fat and kilocalories, and moderate to high in dietary fibre and nutrition, or they have been modified to make them that way. The modified recipes taste good, but slightly different, as well they should. In many of the recipes, fat and kilocalories have been cut by 25-40 percent. Wherever possible, nutrient content and fibre content have been increased. Added fats (cooking oils) and added sodium (salt and salty condiments) have been cut 50 percent in many cases. And, added sugar has been kept very low.

Fatty, energy-rich and nutrient-poor ingredients have been eliminated and replaced with more wholesome ingredients. Saturated fats have been replaced with polyunsaturated and monounsaturated fats. Fatty cuts of meat have been replaced with lean meats, poultry, fish and shellfish, and vegetable protein replaces meat protein in many dishes.

Unwholesome cooking methods have also been eliminated. Foods are quick-fried in a very small quantity of fat, or poached, steamed, baked, grilled, boiled or double-boiled. Some dishes simply call for "frying" in a few drops of oil brushed over a non-stick pan.

Certain categories of Asian foods have been omitted because they cannot be appropriately modified. Things like Indian sweets, *kuih-kuih* and several popular Chinese sweets have been replaced with high-fibre, low-fat, low-sugar international recipes (for the cook who experiments with the healthy elements of foreign cuisines). On the other hand, certain cuisines have been highlighted because they naturally follow good nutritional guidelines (see below). Thus, you will find a higher number of Indian dishes.

If you're a traditionalist who believes in following original recipes and preserving their original taste, then perhaps these recipes are not for you. But, if you're like most modern Asian readers, you have a deep respect for the culinary traditions of the past, but an equally strong desire to live a long and healthy life. This book is for those of you who want both good taste and good health from familiar Asian dishes.

Nutritional Guidelines

The recipes follow the nutritional guidelines given in *The Complete Asian Health and Diet Plan*. Briefly, they are:

1. **Eat a wide variety of foods every day from these food groups:**
   vegetables and fruits
   cereals, grains, noodles and breads
   meats, poultry, fish, shellfish, eggs, legumes and dhal
   milk, cheese, yoghurt, pannir, channa and curd

2. **Maintain your ideal weight.**
   The recipes are all reduced or low in kilocalories and fat. They can help you lose fat weight slowly, safely and permanently. (Don't forget that safe, regular exercise also plays a vital role in maintaining ideal weight.)

3. **Avoid too much fat, saturated fat and cholesterol.**
   Many of the recipes fall within the range of 20-25 percent of kilocalories from fat — the recommended range for Singaporeans. (To determine the percentage of fat in the dishes, just multiply the total grams of fat by nine and divide by the total kilocalories.) Refer to the nutritional chart on each page for information regarding the fat content for each dish.

4. **Eat foods with adequate starch and fibre. Eat more fresh or raw foods and fewer processed foods.**
   The recipes pay particular attention to fibre and complex carbohydrate content. I recommend aiming for between 30 and 40 grams of fibre each day. (See the chart on each page for the fibre content of each dish.)

5. **Cut down on sugar.**
   Added sugar has been kept to a minimum. Although I've included recipes for biscuits and sweets, I've modified them so they are lighter and less sweet than most desserts.

6. **Cut down on salt, salty condiments and table sauces.**
   These have been held to a minimum in all the recipes. Some recipes call for no added sodium, and almost all have no more than ½ teaspoon of added salt. Experts consider between 1,100 and 3,300 milligrams of sodium per day as safe, although we don't really need that much. Use the information in the charts on each page to determine how much sodium the recipes contain.

7. **If you must drink alcohol, do so in moderation.**
   Very small amounts of wine have been used in some recipes.

Recipe Key

What makes this cookbook special is the nutritional information given with each recipe. The chart at the top of each page provides vital information on each dish: the number of kilocalories (kcals) it contains, the fat content (in grams), the fibre content (in grams), the sodium content (in milligrams) and the cholesterol content (also in milligrams). Information has been calculated for the total recipe, as well as for one portion out of four, six, eight or 10 portions, depending upon the number of eaters. (The dishes can, of course, be divided into more or fewer portions, depending on the number of eaters and the other dishes served.) In other words, if you are making Reduced-Fat Chicken Rice (see page 16) for four people, each serving will have 624 kilocalories; if you are cooking for six, each will have only 416 kilocalories. The total number of kilocalories for both the chicken and the rice is 2497.

All figures in the charts have been rounded up to whole numbers unless values are less than one. Calculations for all ingredients are based on standard sizes. To provide the reader with the most accurate nutritional information available, weights and other values have been taken from textbooks or calculated through practical experiments. So, nutritional data based on recipes cooked in your own home could vary slighly from the information provided in the charts.

Other nutritional information — like vitamin and mineral content, whether or not the dish is rich in protein or beta-carotene (the precursor of vitamin A), high in carbohydrate and low in kilocalories and fat, for instance — follows each chart. For the most part, dishes are listed by their popular local names. Ingredients are given in English first, and are often followed by their common Chinese or Malay names. If in doubt, refer to the chart at the back of the book for a list of the English, Chinese and Malay names of foods commonly eaten in Asia. On each page, I've also included the ethnic group the dish derives from and the number of people the recipe serves.

Ingredients have been given in both metric and Imperial measurements. In most cases, the metric measurement precedes the Imperial measurement — except in reference to cups. The cup measurement I have used throughout is the standard, eight-ounce American cup, which is commonly used in this area, and easier to work with than other measuring devices. Wherever applicable, I have included the liquid measurement equivalent in litres and millilitres. (If you don't have a standard American cup, you can use an English breakfast cup. For cooking purposes, the difference is negligible. The nutritional values, however, will change because an English cup contains 10 ounces.)

I have also used the standard American measuring tablespoon and teaspoon, as these are also easier to manipulate. There are 16 U.S. tablespoons and 48 U.S. teaspoons to a standard, eight-ounce U.S. cup. All teaspoon and tablespoon measurements are level. In addition, oven temperatures have been given in Celsius, Fahrenheit and Gas Regulo.

Most of the ingredients in my Asian recipes are freely available in local markets and supermarkets. In a few of the international recipes, I have used ingredients (e.g. sunflower seeds and unsulphured molasses) that are available in health food stores. In some cases, substitutions have been suggested after those ingredients that are difficult to find. Finally, to simplify the cooking steps, I have given chopping, dicing, slicing and other instructions in the list of ingredients.

The following abbreviations have been used throughout the book:

kilocalorie — kcal	cup — C
milligram — mg	tablespoon — T
kilogram — kg	teaspoon — tsp
gram — g	inch — "
centimetre — cm	pound — lb
litre — L	ounces — oz
millilitre — ml	

Healthy Eating and Shopping

The following diagram is a quick guide to what you should and should not eat. Refer to it before doing your marketing and before planning a week's menu for your family.

The foods under the "Eat Frequently" section are very rich in nutrition and belong on your list of healthy staples. Try to include a wide variety of them in every week's marketing. Many of the fruits and vegetables in this section are rich in vitamin C and should be eaten freely. The dark green and deep yellow vegetables and fruits are also rich in beta-carotene, the precursor of vitamin A, and should also be eaten as often as possible.

Fresh soyabean products, *dhal*, beans and peas are nutritional superstars, but avoid the deep-fried or salted soyabean products. Wholegrain cereals, grains, breads and noodles can be eaten liberally, but low-fat dairy products and lean meat, poultry and fish should only be eaten in moderation. Try to limit your intake of fats and oils as much as possible.

amaranth
apples   apricot   asparagus
beets   belimbing   berries   bittergourd
bananas   bean sprouts   beet greens   black beans
bran   bran flakes   brinjal   broad beans   brown rice
broccoli   buckwheat   cabbage   cantaloupe   cauliflower
carrots   celery   chapatis   chard   cherries   chillies   chickory
chye sim   coriander   corn   cracked wheat   capsicum   cucumber
dates   dried beans and peas   drumstick leaves and pods   dhal
endive   escarole   fruit juices   fungus   garlic   grapefruit   green beans
grapes   green peas   guava   hairy cucumber   honeydew melon
jackfruit   jujubes   kailan   kidney beans   kiwi   kangkong   kedondong
longans   leeks   lemon   **Eat Frequently**   lettuce   longbeans   lime
loquat   lima beans   lychee   mango   mangosteen   mata kuching   millet
mint   muskmelon   mustard greens   persimmon   passionfruit   peaches
papaya   pineapple   pinto beans   pumpkin   oatmeal   onions   pomelo
oranges   plain rice porridge   pai tsai   pears   navy beans   pak choy
plums   potatoes   radish   raisins   rambutan   raspberries   red beans
rhubarb   seaweeds   soursop   spinach pasta   strawberries
spinach   star fruit   sweet potatoes   kumquat   lady's fingers
shallots   tempeh   tomatoes watercress   watermelon
tofu   wholewheat breads   wholegrain cereals
wholegrain pasta   wholegrain breads
wheat germ   winter squash   yam
yellow cucumber

Eat Rarely

alcoholic beverages
butter   cheese cake   chilli oil
cheese puffs   chocolate   coconut
coconut cream   coconut milk   corn oil
cream   custard pie   deep-fried foods
doughnuts   french fries   fried onion rings
non-dairy creamer   gula melaka   ice cream   lard
eclairs   ghee   kuih-kuih   non-dairy toppings
oil   salad dressings   pastries   peanut oil
mayonnaise   olive oil   polyunsaturated, soft margarine
pecan pie   potato chips   salad cream   sesame oil
serikaya   olives   soyabean oil
sweet rolls   sour cream
whipped cream

Eat in Moderation

bluefish
buttermilk   catfish   clams
chicken   cod   cottage cheese
crab   crayfish   skim-milk yoghurt
evaporated skim-milk   durian   sole
flounder   frog's legs   haddock
ikan merah   ikan tenggiri   lean beef
lean lamb   lean veal   lean pork   lobster
low-fat milk   mackerel
low-fat cheeses   panir   low-fat yoghurt
miso   oysters   perch   pike   pomfret
skim-milk   part-skim mozzarella cheese
prawns   ricotta cheese   salmon
sardines   scallops   sea bass
squab   squid   turkey
skim-milk cottage cheese
tuna in water

Eat Only Occasionally

almonds
bacon   barbecue sauce
belacan   blue cheese   bologna
brains   brazil nuts   brie cheese
candlenuts   charcoal-broiled meats and fish
cashew nuts   chestnuts   chilli sauce   cincaluk
cheddar cheese   cream cheese   curry puffs   duck
dried prawns   duck eggs   fatty beef   fatty lamb
eel   fatty pork   fatty veal   filberts   fish sauce
fish roe   frankfurters   fried ikan bilis   goose liver   ham
goose   lake trout   herring   kidney
liver   liverwurst   oyster sauce
mutton   packet noodles   luncheon meats   hen eggs
peanut butter   peanuts   packet soups   pepperoni
pistachio nuts   plum sauce   pecans
rainbow trout   salami   preserved vegetables
swiss cheese   sesame seeds   salted eggs   salted fish
soup cubes   sunflower seeds   soyasauce
taucheo   tinned curries   sausage
walnuts   whole-milk yoghurt   tuna in oil
whole milk

Making Your Own Recipes Healthier

The nutritional principles in this book can be applied to almost any recipe to make it healthier. To modify your own recipes:

1. Cut total fat.
— Choose lean meats and poultry and avoid fatty cuts.
— Remove all visible fats from meats and poultry. Trim fats from meats before cooking. Skin chicken before cooking, and remove all the fat found under the skin and in the body cavity.
— Plan ahead when you make soups, stocks and stews. After cooking, let the liquid cool, then refrigerate until all the fats have solidified on the surface. Remove and discard all the fat, then reheat and serve.
— Avoid or sharply cut down on the use of luncheon and processed meats, which are high in fat and kilocalories.
— When buying tinned fish — tuna, mackerel, sardines — drain the oily sauces, and rinse off any excess oil with plain water. Naturally fatty fish like mackerel, tuna and salmon can help lower the risk of heart disease; what you don't need however, is the added oil used in packing them.
— Switch from whole milk to skim-milk and eliminate cream.
— Eliminate oily, bottled salad dressings and creams. Substitute low-fat commercial dressings, or make your own with skim-milk yoghurt, herbs, vinegar and a very small amount of good quality olive oil for flavour.
— Use skim-milk yoghurt instead of yoghurt made from whole milk.
— Do not deep-fry or pan-fry foods. "Sauté" in salt-free chicken broth and "fry" in a non-stick pan lightly brushed with a few drops of polyunsaturated vegetable oil.
— Choose boiling, double-boiling, steaming, grilling, broiling, and baking over frying and braising.
— Try using no more than 1 to 1 ½ tablespoons of added fat (per dish of 4-6 portions) to fry *rempahs, masalas* and seasonings like onions, garlic and ginger.
— When steaming fish, use only a few drops of polyunsaturated or monounsaturated vegetable oil. Season fish with broth, a small amount of soyasauce, garlic, ginger, chillies and spring onions.
— Drain fried foods on kitchen paper towels; skim visible fats from all cooked dishes.

2. Cut saturated fat and cholesterol.
— Cut down sharply on hen and duck eggs, liver, kidney, brains and prawns.
— Cut down on fatty red meats, and increase use of vegetable proteins like bean curd, soyabean products, beans, peas and *dhal*.
— Eliminate the use of ghee, butter and lard. Substitute moderate amounts of polyunsaturated and monounsaturated vegetable oils (soyabean, peanut, corn and olive oils) and soft margarines made from polyunsaturated vegetable oils.
— Sharply cut down on the use of coconut milk and coconut cream. Many Indian curries can be prepared using skim-milk yoghurt instead of coconut. Many Malay and Indonesian dishes can be prepared using tamarind *(assam)* instead of coconut milk *(santan)*. If coconut milk is absolutely necessary in a dish, try using ¼ the amount called for — just to give the flavour. Make up the remaining ¾ with evaporated low-fat milk mixed with water, or skim-milk.
— If you are a cheese eater, cut down sharply on hard and creamy cheeses. Better choices are skim-milk cottage cheese, feta cheese and mozzarella.
— Substitute high-fibre, low-fat, low-sugar sweets and biscuits for coconut-rich, fat-rich, high-kilocalorie *kuih-kuih* and desserts.

3. Increase dietary fibre.
— Increase your intake of *dhal*, beans and peas. Try having one or two vegetarian meals each week — featuring a soyabean, *dhal* or bean dish, a grain dish like brown rice or *chapatis*, a dish of deep green or yellow orange vegetables, and perhaps a yoghurt or cheese dish. (See recipes on pages 60, 61, 74, 75, 91, 114, 66, 68, 146 and 108 for some good suggestions.)
— Switch from soft, white bread to wholegrain breads and rolls.
— Add a moderate amount of *dhal*, beans and peas to soups and stews.
— Add high-fibre vegetables and fruits to your recipes.
— Choose whole fruits and vegetables over fruit and vegetable juices.
— Eat a wide variety of fruits and vegetables and have a serving of each at every meal.
— Substitute fresh fruits, vegetables and wholegrain breads and sweets for sugary, fatty snacks.

— Try raw vegetable salads combining a wide variety of greens and other vegetables — radishes, tomatoes, grated carrots, shredded cabbage, cooked beans, cooked corn kernels, shredded red or white onions, and green or red capsicums.

— Choose oatmeal served with skim-milk and fresh fruit for a breakfast dish instead of sugary breakfast cereals. Choose wholegrain, low-fat, low-sugar, high-fibre commercially prepared breakfast cereals.

— Include a moderate amount of dried fruits in your diet, e.g., dried apricots, dried figs and dried apples.

— Eat brown, unpolished rice instead of white rice several times a week. (See the comparison between the vitamin contents of brown and white rice below.) If you find it hard to adjust to the nutty, slightly crunchy flavour of 100 percent unpolished rice, try combining half brown rice with half polished rice. Gradually increase the proportion of brown rice until you become accustomed.

Vitamin Content: Brown Rice versus White Rice

	brown	white
thiamine	0.34	0.07
riboflavin	0.05	0.03
niacin	4.7	1.6
pyridoxine	1.03	0.45
pantothenic acid	1.5	0.75
folic acid	0.02	0.016
biotin	0.012	0.005
inositol	119	10
choline	12	59

As you can see, brown rice is higher in vitamins than white rice. (Figures are in milligrams per 100 grams. Source: Stanley F. Brockington and Vincent J. Kelly, in "Rice: Chemistry and Technology," ed. D.F. Houston, St. Paul, Minnesota: American Association of Cereal Chemists, 1972)

4. Cut sodium.

— Cut down sharply on added salt in recipes.

— Cut down sharply on soyabean sauce, fish sauce, oyster sauce, chilli sauce, catsup, salted, fermented soyabeans *(taucheo)*, preserved soyabean curd *(foo yu)*, salted soyabeans, brown bean sauce, *miso* and *belacan*.

— Cut down sharply on salted, preserved vegetables like *kiam chye* and Sichuan vegetables.

— Cut down sharply on salted, preserved fish, meat and poultry.

— If using packet noodles, discard the salty condiments, and season the noodles with home-made broth, chillies, lightly fried or raw garlic, chopped coriander, spring onions, and a very small amount of soyabean sauce. Add fresh vegetables like *kailan* or *kangkong* for additional flavour and fibre.

— Cut down sharply on processed foods — potato crisps, salted peanuts, cheese, ham, tinned products like soups, vegetables, stews, curries and tomato sauce.

— Eliminate monosodium glutamate (MSG).

— Eliminate soup cubes and salty, MSG-laden packet stocks. Make your own healthy stocks from fresh vegetables simmered with fat-free chicken, meat or fish bones.

— Buy fresh or frozen vegetables. If you must use tinned vegetables, rinse them thoroughly to lower the salt content.

— Read labels. Sodium is contained in foods with sodium ascorbate, baking powder, baking soda, sodium saccharin, sodium phosphate, sodium nitrate and sodium bicarbonate.

— Whenever possible, eat freshly prepared, home-cooked meals. Restaurant and hawker meals are high in MSG and sodium.

— Use ginger, garlic, spring onions, lime juice, ground fresh chillies, vinegar and herbs to season food instead of salt and salty table sauces.

— Be patient. At first your tastebuds may miss salt. But in a remarkably short time, you will adjust. When I first began testing these recipes, I missed the taste of salt terribly. After two weeks though, even ½ teaspoon of added salt or 1 teaspoon of soyabean sauce (in a recipe for 4-6) tasted too salty.

5. Cut down on sugar.

There is a place for sugar in our diets. It is a valuable source of energy when we eat it in its natural form in milk, fruits and other unrefined foods. But adding excess, refined sugar to our diets can lead to overweight and dental decay, and it increases the risk of diabetes. Most importantly, excess sugar fills us up with "empty" kilocalories so we eat less nutrient-rich foods.

— Eat fresh fruits when you want a sweet snack.

— Choose tinned fruit packed in natural juice, instead of heavy syrup.

— In food centres and restaurants, choose unsweetened fruit juices.

— Cut down sharply on sweetened soft drinks. A typical soft drink contains 9-12 teaspoons of sugar in a 355 ml (12 oz) serving.

— Instead of sugary soft drinks, mix ½ fresh fruit juice with ½ low-sodium mineral water, club soda or plain water.

— Use pureed fresh fruits instead of jams, syrups and treacles. (See the recipe for Strawberry Sauce on page 85.)

— Choose unsweetened, commercially prepared cereals; add fresh fruit or moderate amounts of raisins for sweetness.

— Choose plain, skim-milk yoghurt and add your own pureed fresh fruit, instead of prepared fruit yoghurts loaded with syrupy preserves.

— Don't bribe or reward children with sugary treats — or foods of any kind. A hug and a kiss costs nothing and is a much better reward.

6. Guard against unnecessary vitamin loss.

— To get the best nutritive value from vegetables, eat them raw whenever possible.

— Vegetables that must be cooked should be prepared and eaten soon after purchasing.

— Don't soak vegetables in water. By discarding it you lose minerals and water-soluble vitamins.

— Cook vegetables as briefly as possible — heat can destroy some of the vitamins. To reduce vitamin C loss, keep the pot covered during the cooking.

— Steam vegetables instead of boiling.

— Don't add baking powder to vegetables — it destroys the vitamin C.

— Don't defrost meats and fish in pans of water — minerals and water-soluble vitamins will be lost. Do use meat juices from defrosting in your soup, stew or curry.

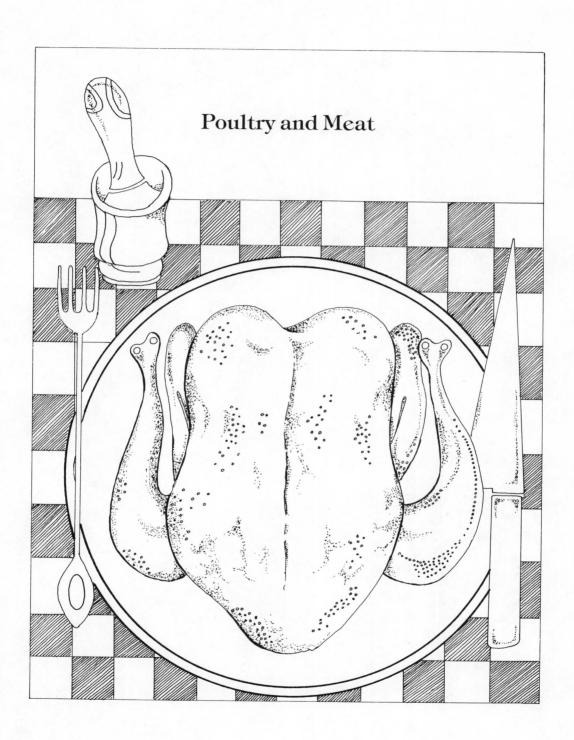

Poultry and Meat

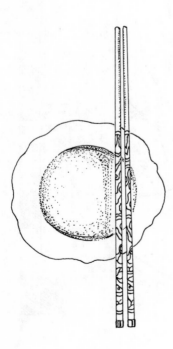

CHINESE

Star Anise Chicken in Soyasauce

(serves 4-6)

	total	1 of 4 portions	1 of 6 portions
kcal	1920	480	320
fat (g)	67	17	11
sodium (mg)	13,240	3310	2207
dietary fibre (g)	1	.3	.2
cholesterol (mg)	1077	269	180

This is a simple, delicious dish. The sauce is rather high in sodium, so be sure to use only the amount indicated at serving time. Like all chicken dishes, this one is an excellent source of protein and phosphorus, and a fair source of thiamine, riboflavin and iron.

1 whole chicken (about 1.7 kg or 3¾ lb),
    washed and dried
2 C (500 ml) water
1 C (250 ml) light soyasauce
1 C (250 ml) dark soyasauce
¼ C (65 ml) Chinese rice wine

2.5 cm (1″) piece fresh ginger
4 whole star anise
2 T sugar (or equivalent rock sugar)
1 tsp sesame oil

1. *In a heavy pot just large enough to fit the chicken snugly, heat the water, soyasauces, wine, ginger, star anise and sugar until boiling. Add chicken, lying on its side. (Note: liquid should reach ⅔ up the side of the chicken when it's lying on its back.) Return to the boil, then reduce heat to low, and simmer for 5 minutes. Turn the chicken over to its other side, and simmer another 5 minutes. Turn breast side up, cover pot, turn off the heat, and let the chicken rest for another 30-40 minutes, until the thighs are cooked through.*

2. *Drain the chicken, remove the skin, pat dry, and brush with sesame oil. Cut into bite-sized pieces, and moisten with ¼ C of the cooking liquid. Serve at room temperature.*

Note: The sauce in which the chicken is cooked may be used for red-cooked dishes. It will keep for 2 weeks in the refrigerator and up to 3 months in the freezer.

CHINESE

Reduced-Fat Chicken Rice

(serves 4-6)

	total	1 of 4 portions	1 of 6 portions
kcal	2497	624	416
fat (g)	56	14	9
sodium (mg)	2813	703	469
dietary fibre (g)	10	3	2
cholesterol (mg)	637	159	106

A generous portion of Reduced-Fat Chicken Rice contains 624 kilocalories and 14 grams of fat, compared to a S$2 hawker serving which has 861 kilocalories and 31 grams of fat. This is because the rice in my recipe is less rich and oily than the rice in the traditional recipe. Although it may be a new experience to remove the chicken skin, the savings in fat and kilocalories make it worth trying. The chicken is an excellent source of protein and phosphorus, and a fair source of thiamine, riboflavin and iron. (Note: the nutritional information covers both chicken and rice.)

1 whole, very fresh chicken (1 kg or 2.2 lb)
1 tsp Chinese rice wine
1½ T light soyasauce
1.25 cm (½") piece ginger

2 spring onions
1 tsp sesame oil
½ tsp salt

1. *Season the chicken cavity with rice wine and soyasauce; put the ginger and spring onions into the cavity.*

2. *Choose a saucepan in which the chicken will fit snugly; fill the pan ⅔ full with water and bring to a rolling boil. Place the chicken in breast up, turn off the heat and cover the pan.*

3. *When the chicken has stood for five minutes, lift it out and carefully drain the water from its cavity. Return the chicken to the water and let stand again. Repeat this procedure 3 more times during the next hour so that the chicken cooks evenly, inside and out. At the end of 30 minutes, turn on the heat and bring the water almost to a boil. Turn off heat and let the chicken continue to stand. When the hour is up, drain the chicken (but save the water for the rice), remove all skin and visible fat, pat dry with paper towels, rub with the sesame oil and salt and let rest for 20 minutes. Then cut into bite-sized pieces. Serve with rice and Chilli and Ginger Sauce (see recipe next page).*

Salt-Baked Chicken with Sesame and Peanut Oil Sauce, page 18

Bulgogi (Korean Barbecued Beef Slices), page 37, and Crispy Pear Salad (Chomuchim), page 156

Thai Thom Yam Soup, page 139, and Prawn and Squid Salad, page 154

Grilled Fish with Chillies, page 46, and Farina with Vegetables (Uppuma), page 118

Chicken Rice:

2 C long-grain rice
about 2½ C (625 ml) chicken stock (from the
    chicken recipe above), with all fat skimmed
    off
1 T soya oil
2 screwpine (*pandan*) leaves, tied into a knot

1. *Wash the rice thoroughly in several changes of cold water, and place in a rice cooker with chicken stock (enough to reach the 2 C mark inside the cooker). Add oil and stir. Place screwpine leaves on top of rice and cook according to rice cooker instructions.*

CHINESE

Chilli and Ginger Sauce

	total
kcal	84
fat (g)	.9
sodium (mg)	14
dietary fibre (g)	23
cholesterol (mg)	0

As well as being a tasty condiment, this sauce has a good amount of beta-carotene (a precursor of vitamin A), potassium and vitamin C. Some people prefer separate chilli and ginger sauces; this version saves time, and cuts kilocalories from fat and sugar.

10 fresh red chillies, sliced
2 cloves garlic
5 cm (2") piece fresh ginger

1 T chicken stock
juice of 2 local limes (*limau kesturi*)
salt

1. *Pound chillies, garlic and ginger. Add chicken stock, lime juice and salt to taste. Serve with Reduced-Fat Chicken Rice.*

Salt-Baked Chicken

(serves 4-6)

	total	1 of 4 portions	1 of 6 portions
kcal	1441	360	240
fat (g)	67	17	11
sodium (mg)	4542	1136	757
dietary fibre (g)	3	.8	.5
cholesterol (mg)	776	194	129

Be sure to wrap the chicken securely in 3 layers of greaseproof paper to prevent the salt from reaching the chicken. Removing the skin before serving cuts down on fat and kilocalories.

1 whole chicken (about 1.2 kg or 2½ lb)
2 tsp ginger juice
2 tsp Chinese rice wine
2 tsp soya oil

2 tsp peanut oil
3 spring onions
3 layers of greaseproof paper
3 kg (about 6½ lb) coarse salt

1. Rub chicken cavity with ginger juice and rice wine. Rub skin with soya and peanut oils and put the spring onions inside the cavity. Wrap the chicken securely in greaseproof paper.

2. Meantime, heat the salt in a large covered kuali or wok for 10 minutes, until very hot. Carefully remove half the salt and bury the chicken breast up in remaining salt. Then cover chicken completely with the salt just removed. Cover the kuali tightly and cook over very low heat for one hour.

3. Remove paper wrapping, remove skin, and cut chicken into serving pieces; serve with Sesame and Peanut Oil Sauce (see next recipe).

Sesame and Peanut Oil Sauce

	total
kcal	423
fat (g)	42
sodium (mg)	1054
dietary fibre (g)	2
cholesterol (mg)	0

2.5 cm (1") piece fresh ginger, finely minced
1 spring onion, cut into very fine rings
1½ T peanut oil
1½ T sesame oil
1 T oyster sauce

1. Combine all ingredients, mix well and place into individual sauce dishes.

CHINESE

Claypot Chicken

(serves 4-6)

	total	1 of 4 portions	1 of 6 portions
kcal	2000	500	333
fat (g)	40	10	7
sodium (mg)	2072	518	345
dietary fibre (g)	12	3	2
cholesterol (mg)	492	123	82

This is a typical home-style dish — simple, filling, hearty, and deeply satisfying. It's also a convenient one-dish meal. Fat and kilocalories have been cut in this version, which is rich in protein, carbohydrates, niacin, riboflavin, iron, phosphorus and thiamine. Cooking over very low heat brings best results.

Marinade:

2 T oyster sauce
1 T thick black soyasauce
1 tsp Chinese rice wine
1 tsp cornflour
½ tsp sesame oil
½ tsp sugar

750 g (about 1½ lb) chicken pieces, skinned, all fat removed, and cut into 12 pieces
4 dried black mushrooms, soaked until soft and stems removed
1½ C long-grain rice, washed thoroughly until water runs clear
2 C (500 ml) water
4 thin slices fresh ginger
1 Chinese sausage (*lap cheong*), cut into 4 cm (1½") diagonal pieces

1. *Mix together marinade ingredients and marinate chicken pieces and mushrooms at least one hour.*

2. *Put rice and water into a claypot, cover and bring to a boil. Cook rapidly until the water is evaporated and little steam holes appear on the surface of the rice.*

3. *Remove chicken and mushrooms from marinade and place on top of the rice. Add the ginger slices and sausage. Cover the pot securely, and cook over very low heat about 45 minutes, until chicken is very tender. Be careful not to burn the rice. Serve directly from the claypot.*

CHINESE

Bon Bon Chicken with Sesame Sauce

(serves 4-6)

	total	1 of 4 portions	1 of 6 portions
kcal	982	246	164
fat (g)	70	18	12
sodium (mg)	2026	507	338
dietary fibre (g)	11	3	2
cholesterol (mg)	165	41	28

There's a lovely combination of textures in this smooth, light dish. It's also quite low in kilocalories and relatively low in fat. Assemble the dish at the last moment before serving to retain the crunchiness of the fried noodles. If you use peanut butter instead of sesame paste, the dish will have a total of 960 kilocalories, 67 grams of fat, 2225 milligrams of sodium, 5 grams of dietary fibre and no cholesterol.

30 g (1 oz) transparent noodles (*tang hoon*)
oil for deep frying
170 g (6 oz) boneless chicken breast
2 T Chinese sesame paste or smooth peanut
    butter
3 T prepared tea
2 T light soyasauce

2 T light rice vinegar
2 tsp sesame oil
1 tsp sugar
½ tsp ground cayenne pepper
1 cucumber, peeled, seeded and shredded
2 spring onions, minced

1. *Divide transparent noodles into two batches. Soak half in hot water for 30 minutes. Deep-fry the rest for about 3 seconds, until they puff up and turn white and crisp. Drain on paper towels, patting off all visible oil, and spread on a serving plate.*

2. *Poach the chicken breast in water for about 8 minutes, or until the meat is firm and white but not dry. Shred the meat into thin strips.*

3. *Mix sesame paste/peanut butter with tea, then add soyasauce, vinegar, oil, sugar and cayenne pepper. Toss this mixture with the chicken shreds.*

4. *Arrange a layer of cucumber strips over the fried noodles; top with softened noodles, then with chicken mixture. Garnish with spring onion and serve chilled or at room temperature.*

INDIAN

Tandoori Chicken

(serves 4-6)

	total	1 of 4 portions	1 of 6 portions
kcal	1787	447	298
fat (g)	61	15	10
sodium (mg)	2009	502	335
dietary fibre (g)	9	2	2
cholesterol (mg)	973	243	162

This classic dish is excellent served warm from the oven, at room temperature, or served the second day, when the spices have penetrated the chicken even further. It's rich in protein, and a good source of phosphorus, thiamine, riboflavin, and calcium. (Tip: because of the long preparation time, it is a good idea to double the recipe. Tandoori chicken disappears quickly, even in small families.)

1.5 kg (3 lb) chicken
¼ C (65 ml) fresh lemon juice
½ tsp salt
1 tsp saffron threads, soaked in 3 T boiling water
1 C plain, skim-milk yoghurt
50 g (2 oz) onion, pounded

4 cloves garlic, pounded
2 tsp ginger juice
1 T tomato puree
2 tsp ground coriander
1 tsp ground chilli (cayenne)
2 tsp ground mustard
1 tsp sugar
150 g (5 oz) onion rings

1. Skin, clean and wash chicken. Pat completely dry inside and out. Truss the chicken. Make 2 slits in each thigh and breast, about 1.25 cm (½") deep. Rub in the lemon juice and salt, pour the saffron and its liquid over the chicken, and allow to marinate for one hour.

2. Mix all the remaining ingredients except the onion rings, and spread the mixture over the chicken, pressing it into the slits in the breasts and thighs. Cover, and allow to marinate 6 hours at room temperature, or 8 hours in the refrigerator. Turn the chicken in the marinade every hour or so.

3. Preheat the oven to 205°C (400°F or Gas Regulo 8) and place the chicken breast side down on a rack in a baking pan. Pour the marinade over the chicken, and roast uncovered for 10 minutes. Then reduce heat to 190°C (375°F or Gas Regulo 7), turn the chicken breast side up and spread the onion rings over the chicken; roast an additional 20 minutes, or until the thighs test done when pierced with a skewer. (Be sure to test chicken, as cooking time will vary depending on the size of the bird and the eccentricities of your oven.) Traditional garnishes include slivered onions, quartered tomatoes and lemons, radishes and green chillies.

Chicken Cardamom

(serves 4-6)

	total	1 of 4 portions	1 of 6 portions
kcal	2064	516	344
fat (g)	86	22	14
sodium (mg)	1998	500	333
dietary fibre (g)	10	3	2
cholesterol (mg)	973	243	162

This is a marvelously fragrant, delicate dish, best served with plain rice or *chapatis*, and a dry vegetable curry. It is rich in protein and a good source of calcium, riboflavin, thiamine and iron.

1.5 kg (3 lb) chicken
½ tsp salt
1 C plain, skim-milk yoghurt
seeds of 12 cardamom pods, pounded
3.75 cm (1½") piece fresh ginger, pounded
4 cloves garlic, pounded
1 tsp aniseed, ground
1 tsp ground chilli (cayenne)

2 T soya oil
1 stick cinnamon
2 cloves
3 onions (about 400 g or 14 oz), finely
   chopped
½ tsp saffron, soaked in 3 T boiling water
½ C (125 ml) cold water

1. *Skin, clean, wash, and thoroughly dry chicken. Rub salt over the chicken, and place in a bowl. Combine the yoghurt, cardamom, ginger, garlic, aniseed and chilli and mix well. Rub mixture over all parts of the chicken and inside the body cavity. Marinate, covered, at room temperature for 4 hours.*

2. *In a kuali or karhai with a lid, heat the oil over medium heat, add the cinnamon and cloves and stir. Then add the onions, and fry for 7 minutes, until lightly browned. Add the chicken, its marinade, the saffron and its liquid. Cook the chicken gently for 10 minutes, turning frequently, until the oil rises to the surface of the masala. Stir in the cold water, bring to a boil, and immediately reduce the heat to low. Cover and simmer gently for 30 to 35 minutes until the chicken is tender but not falling apart.*

INDIAN

Chicken Korma

(serves 4-6)

	total	1 of 4 portions	1 of 6 portions
kcal	2420	605	403
fat (g)	102	26	17
sodium (mg)	2019	505	337
dietary fibre (g)	12	3	2
cholesterol (mg)	986	247	164

My version of this popular, mild chicken curry omits the coconut milk and cream, and uses skim-milk yoghurt and evaporated milk for richness. The savings in fat and kilocalories are significant, and there's plenty of good, smooth taste in this light version. It's also rich in protein, and a good source of thiamine, calcium, iron, riboflavin and other B vitamins.

1 whole chicken, about 1.5 kg (3 lb)
1 T ginger juice
½ C plain, skim-milk yoghurt
1½ tsp chilli powder (cayenne)
2 tsp ground coriander
4 onions (about 400 g or 14 oz), slivered
½ tsp sugar
½ tsp salt
2 T soya oil

2 sticks cinnamon
seeds of 6 green cardamom pods, crushed
5 cloves garlic, pounded
1 T almonds, ground
2 tsp yellow raisins, ground
¼ C (65 ml) evaporated milk
2 C (500 ml) boiling water
15 shallots, peeled

1. *Skin, clean, wash, and thoroughly dry chicken. Cut into 10 pieces. Combine ginger juice, yoghurt, chilli powder, ground coriander, 1½ T onion slivers, sugar and salt, and add chicken pieces. Marinate 4 hours at room temperature.*

2. *Heat the oil over medium heat and add the cinnamon, cardamom, remaining slivered onions and garlic. Fry until onions are lightly brown. Add the almonds and raisins, and a little water, and fry for 2 minutes. Then add chicken pieces, stir to coat well, and cover the pan. Cook over medium heat, covered, for 5 minutes, stirring occasionally to avoid burning.*

3. *When the chicken is dry, add evaporated milk and boiling water. Simmer, covered, until chicken is tender. Add the shallots, and continue to cook, uncovered, until the sauce is very thick and quite dry.*

Chicken Masala

(serves 4-6)

	.total	1 of 4 portions	1 of 6 portions
kcal	2127	532	355
fat (g)	85	21	14
sodium (mg)	1126	282	188
dietary fibre (g)	32	8	5
cholesterol (mg)	973	243	162

This dish is a good source of protein, B vitamins and iron.

1 stick cinnamon, crushed
4 dried red chillies, seeded and pounded
4 cloves garlic, pounded
8 cloves, pounded
3.75 cm (1½") piece ginger, pounded
1 T white poppy seeds, pounded
1 T ground cumin
¼ tsp garam masala

1 tsp salt
3-4 T water
1½ T soya oil
250 g (8 oz or about 2) onions, peeled, halved and slivered
1.5 kg (3 lb) chicken, skinned and all visible fat removed
1 C plain, skim-milk yoghurt
1 C (250 ml) water

1. *Pound together cinnamon, chillies, garlic, cloves, ginger, poppy seeds, cumin, garam masala, ½ tsp salt, and 3-4 T water, to moisten. Heat the oil in a karhai or kuali, and fry the onions and the remaining ½ tsp salt for 7 minutes, or until golden brown. Drain the oil from the onions, pound them to a paste and add them to the* masala.

2. *Clean, wash, and thoroughly dry the chicken. Make 2 slits about 1.25 cm (½") deep and 3.75 cm (1½") long in each breast, leg and thigh. Rub the* masala *into the chicken, inside and out, pressing it deeply into the slits, and over all its surfaces. Cover and marinate 2 hours.*

3. *Place the chicken and marinade in a pot with a lid; add yoghurt and water. Bring to a boil over high heat while stirring constantly and turning chicken to coat evenly. Reduce heat to low, cover and simmer for 35 minutes, until chicken is tender, but not falling apart.*

INDIAN

Roast Chicken Parsi-Style

(serves 4-6)

	total	1 of 4 portions	1 of 6 portions
kcal	1483	371	247
fat (g)	38	10	6
sodium (mg)	1839	460	307
dietary fibre (g)	32	8	5
cholesterol (mg)	647	162	108

This is a subtly spiced twice-cooked dish, quite rich in protein, and a good source of thiamine, B vitamins, iron and riboflavin. A combination of skim-milk and evaporated milk replaces high-fat and high-kilocalorie coconut milk in the original recipe. Serve with *chapatis* (see recipe page 114), brown rice or spiced potatoes, and an Indian salad (see pages 91, 71 and 146).

1 kg (2.2 lb) chicken, skinned and halved lengthwise
½ tsp salt
½ C skim-milk powder mixed with 1 ½ C (375 ml) water
½ C (125 ml) evaporated milk
1 stalk lemon grass, crushed
4 fresh red chillies

6 cloves garlic
5 cm (2") piece ginger
½ tsp saffron soaked in 2 T boiling water
1 T tomato puree
2 tsp honey
200 g (7 oz or about 2) onions, sliced into rings
juice of 1 lemon

1. *Clean, wash and thoroughly dry chicken. Rub with salt, cover and let stand 2 hours. Then simmer, partially covered, in skim-milk powder mixed with water, evaporated milk and lemon grass until tender and quite dry. Remove chicken.*

2. *Preheat oven to 205°C (400°F or Gas Regulo 8). Pound together chillies, garlic and ginger; add saffron and its liquid, tomato puree and honey. Place chicken in a baking dish and spread this mixture over both sides. Top with onion rings, and bake 25-30 minutes, until golden brown. Sprinkle chicken with lemon juice and serve.*

INDIAN

Bengali-Style Chicken Curry with Yoghurt

(serves 4-6)

	total	1 of 4 portions	1 of 6 portions
kcal	2156	539	359
fat (g)	79	20	13
sodium (mg)	1961	490	327
dietary fibre (g)	15	4	3
cholesterol (mg)	964	241	161

This very flavourful dish is rich in protein, vitamins C and B6 and beta-carotene, and a good source of thiamine, riboflavin and iron. It is best served with *chapatis* (see recipe page 114) and a deep green or yellow vegetable.

1.5 kg (3 lb) chicken, cleaned, washed, cut in 10 pieces and skinned
2 tsp ground turmeric
½ C plain, skim-milk yoghurt
1 tsp sugar
½ tsp salt
225 g (8 oz) medium potatoes, scrubbed but not peeled, and quartered
1½ T soya oil
½ tsp cumin seed
2 sticks cinnamon
seeds of 4 green cardamom pods

4 cloves garlic, minced
150 g (5 oz or 1 medium) onion, halved and slivered
juice of 1 onion
2 tsp ginger juice
1 T ground chilli (cayenne)
2 tsp ground cumin
3 bay leaves
2 C (500 ml) boiling water
340 g (12 oz or about 4 medium) tomatoes, quartered

1. Marinate chicken in 1 tsp turmeric, yoghurt, sugar and salt for one hour. Rub the potatoes with the remaining turmeric and set aside.

2. Heat the oil in a pan with a lid over medium heat and fry the cumin, cinnamon and cardamom for one minute. Then add the garlic and onion and fry about 7 minutes, until lightly browned. Add chicken and its marinade, onion juice, ginger juice, ground chilli, ground cumin and bay leaves. Blend well, cover, and simmer until liquid is evaporated.

3. Add boiling water and potatoes, and cover and simmer until chicken is nearly cooked — about 20 minutes. Add the tomatoes and cook until chicken is tender. The sauce should be quite thick by this time.

Sumatran-Style Ayam Paggang (Grilled Chicken)

(serves 4-6)

	total	1 of 4 portions	1 of 6 portions
kcal	1199	300	200
fat (g)	50	13	8
sodium (mg)	2567	642	428
dietary fibre (g)	15	4	3
cholesterol (mg)	637	159	106

This dish is remarkably easy to prepare, and absolutely delicious. A simple but healthy standby when time is short, it is also low in kilocalories and fat.

1½ T sweet soyasauce (*kicap manis*)
1 T tamarind (*assam*) mixed with 2½ T water and strained
1 T soya oil

¼ tsp salt
30 g (1 oz or about 3) red chillies, pounded
1 kg (2.2 lb) chicken, quartered, skinned and all visible fat removed

1. Preheat oven grill or charcoal grill. Combine sweet soyasauce, tamarind, soya oil, salt and pounded chillies. Let mixture steep 5 minutes, then use it to marinate the chicken pieces 20 minutes.

2. Grill, basting frequently with marinade until the juices that run from a pricked thigh are yellow, with no trace of blood.

INDONESIAN

Reduced-Fat Ayam Kuning

(serves 4-6)

	total	1 of 4 portions	1 of 6 portions
kcal	2422	606	404
fat (g)	134	34	22
sodium (mg)	1985	496	331
dietary fibre (g)	5	1	.8
cholesterol (mg)	999	250	167

This version has less than half the fat and substantially fewer kilocalories than the traditional recipe, but maintains its smoothness and flavour. It's also a good source of protein, thiamine, niacin, vitamins B6 and B12, pantothenic acid, folacin and choline.

½ tsp ground coriander
½ tsp galingale (*lengkuas*), minced
½ tsp salt
1.5 kg (3 lb) chicken, cut into 10 pieces, skinned and all fat removed
1½ T soya oil
100 g (4 oz or about 1) onion, shredded
4 cloves garlic, pounded

2 candlenuts, pounded
¼ stem lemon grass (*serai*), finely sliced and pounded
1½ tsp ground turmeric
½ C (125 ml) evaporated milk mixed with ¾ C (190 ml) water
½ C (125 ml) thin coconut milk
2 tsp tamarind (*assam*) mixed with 2 T water and strained

1. *Mix coriander, galingale and salt, and rub mixture over chicken. Heat oil over moderate heat and fry onion, garlic, candlenuts and lemon grass until onions are soft and golden brown. Add turmeric and stir; add chicken pieces and stir to coat well.*

2. *Add evaporated milk and water, thin coconut milk and tamarind. Simmer over low heat, stirring occasionally, for about 40-45 minutes until chicken is tender.*

Chicken Salad (Goi Ga)

(serves 4-6)

	total	1 of 4 portions	1 of 6 portions
kcal	1360	340	227
fat (g)	57	14	10
sodium (mg)	644	161	107
dietary fibre (g)	37	9	6
cholesterol (mg)	485	121	81

Vietnamese food is renowned for its use of fresh vegetables and aromatic herbs. An added dividend is that it's generally low in kilocalories and fat. This dish is one of the best examples of the cuisine: it's rich in vitamin C, protein, vitamin B complex and iron.

500 g (1 lb) chicken breast, boned and skinned (yielding about 250 g or ½ lb), poached until just done, and finely shredded

1½ T *nuoc-mam* sauce (see recipe page 41)

200 g (7 oz) white cabbage (not the Chinese variety), finely shredded

150 g (5 oz) red cabbage, finely shredded

8 shallots, shredded

2 fresh red chillies, seeded and finely shredded

2 spring onions, trimmed and finely shredded

1 small bunch mint leaves, stripped from stems and shredded

10 *laksa* leaves, shredded

1 small bunch coriander, stems removed

1 T sugar

2½ T vinegar

2 T roasted peanuts, crushed

1. *Season the shredded chicken with the* nuoc-mam *sauce. Combine with cabbages, shallots, red chillies, spring onion, mint,* laksa *leaves and coriander. (Save some mint and coriander for garnish.) Mix well.*

2. *Dissolve sugar in vinegar, and toss with the shredded ingredients. Adjust seasoning to taste — adding more vinegar, sugar and/or* nuoc-mam, *according to preference. Let the salad sit for 20 minutes before serving. Garnish with mint and coriander sprigs and roasted peanuts.*

Variation: add 3 cloves garlic, shredded, and 20 basil leaves, shredded.

Teriyaki Chicken Thighs

(serves 4-6)

	total	1 of 4 portions	1 of 6 portions
kcal	1664	416	277
fat (g)	35	9	6
sodium (mg)	2871	718	479
dietary fibre (g)	3	.8	.5
cholesterol (mg)	528	132	88

These grilled thighs are plump and succulent, a good source of protein and phosphorus, and a fair source of thiamine.

12 boned, skinned chicken thighs, all visible fat removed
2 C (500 ml) *teriyaki* sauce (see next page)
½ C *teriyaki* glaze (see next page)

4 tsp ground mustard, mixed with enough cold water to form a paste
12 sprigs coriander

1. Marinate the chicken in teriyaki *sauce for 20 minutes. Preheat the oven grill, or light a charcoal grill. Grill or broil 7 cm (3") from the heat for 2 minutes. Dip the chicken thighs into the sauce again and broil the other side for 2-3 minutes. Dip a third time and broil a final 3 minutes, or until the chicken is golden brown, succulent and just done.*

2. Cut the chicken into pieces, and arrange on individual plates, brushing each portion with teriyaki *glaze, and garnishing with a portion of mustard and a coriander sprig.*

Teriyaki Sauce

	total
kcal	844
fat (g)	.2
sodium (mg)	2742
dietary fibre (g)	0
cholesterol (mg)	0

1 C (250 ml) *mirin* (sweet *sake*)
½ C (125 ml) light soyasauce
½ C (125 ml) water
1 C (250 ml) salt-free chicken stock (see recipe page 140)

1. Heat the mirin *in a small saucepan, turn off the heat, carefully ignite the* mirin *with a match, and shake the pan gently until the flame dies out. Stir in the soyasauce, water and stock, and bring to a boil. Cool to room temperature.*

Teriyaki Glaze

	total
kcal	219
fat (g)	.2
sodium (mg)	436
dietary fibre (g)	0
cholesterol (mg)	0

½ C (125 ml) *teriyaki* sauce (see above)
3 tsp sugar
3 tsp cornflour mixed with 1 T cold water

1. *Combine the teriyaki* sauce *and sugar in a small stainless steel saucepan. Bring almost to a boil over moderate heat, then reduce the heat to low and add the cornflour paste. Cook, stirring briskly, until the glaze is syrupy, clear and thick. Pour into a bowl and cool to room temperature.*

Yakitori (Skewered Chicken, Spring Onions and Chicken Livers)

(serves 4)

	total	1 of 4 portions
kcal	1627	407
fat (g)	42	11
sodium (mg)	2622	656
dietary fibre (g)	5	1
cholesterol (mg)	2088	522

This dish is a good source of trace minerals, vitamins A, D, E, and K, B vitamins, and folic acid, as well as being low in kilocalories and fat.

3 T *sake* (rice wine)
½ T light soyasauce
2 tsp sugar
2.5 cm (1") piece ginger, finely sliced
8 chicken livers, trimmed of all fat
4 boned, skinned chicken thighs, all visible fat removed, and cut into 2.5 cm (1") pieces

8 spring onions, cut into 3.75 cm (1 ½") pieces
1 ½ C (375 ml) *teriyaki* sauce (see recipe page 31)
kona sansho (Japanese pepper condiment)

1. Combine the *sake, soyasauce, sugar, ginger and chicken livers; mix well and marinate 6 hours at room temperature. Remove, and cut each liver in half.*

2. *On each of 4 small bamboo skewers, thread 4 chicken liver halves. On each of 8 additional skewers, alternate 4 chunks of chicken with 3 pieces of spring onion. Marinate the skewers in* teriyaki *sauce for 20 minutes.*

3. *Preheat the oven grill, or light a charcoal grill. Grill the skewers 7 cm (3") from the heat for 4 minutes. Dip into the* teriyaki *sauce, and broil the other side for 3 minutes. Dip once more, and broil for an additional 2 minutes.*

4. *Serve sprinkled with* kona sansho, *and moistened with a little of the* teriyaki *marinade.*

Sumatran-Style Ayam Paggang (Grilled Chicken), page 27, Easy Lontong (Compressed Rice), page 92, and Reduced-Fat Pumpkin and Long Bean Curry, page 77

Reduced-Fat Sop Kambing (Lamb Soup), page 132

Low-Fat, High-Fibre Fruit Shakes, page 86

Sambal Udang (Prawns with Chilli), page 54, Sambal Sotong (Chilli Squids), page 57, and Fried Water Convolvulus (Kangkong Tumis Belacan), page 70

NONYA

Ayam Tempra (Chicken in Soyasauce and Lime Juice)

(serves 6-8)

	total	1 of 6 portions	1 of 8 portions
kcal	1684	281	211
fat (g)	72	12	9
sodium (mg)	2397	400	300
dietary fibre (g)	21	4	3
cholesterol (mg)	765	128	96

This dish is very simple to prepare and has a very satisfying flavour. It's low in kilocalories and fat, rich in protein, a good source of phosphorus, a fair source of thiamine and riboflavin, and has some vitamin C and beta-carotene.

2 T soya oil
400 g (14 oz) onion, finely sliced
30 g (1 oz) fresh red chilli, finely sliced
1.2 kg (about 2½ lb) chicken, skinned and cut into 10 pieces

1 T sugar
2 T thick black soyasauce
4 T fresh local lime juice (*limau kesturi*)
1 C (250 ml) water

1. *In a non-stick frying pan or wok, heat oil over moderate heat and fry onions and chilli for 2 minutes; add chicken pieces and fry 10 minutes longer, stirring occasionally. Add sugar and continue to fry for 2 minutes.*

2. *Add the soyasauce, lime juice and water, and simmer, uncovered, until the chicken is tender and the sauce is slightly thickened.*

NONYA

Ayam Sioh (Chicken with Coriander and Tamarind)

(serves 6-8)

	total	1 of 6 portions	1 of 8 portions
kcal	1364	227	171
fat (g)	43	7	5
sodium (mg)	1904	317	238
dietary fibre (g)	.6	.1	.08
cholesterol (mg)	765	128	96

This dish is reduced in fat and kilocalories, but retains the superb flavour of the original. It's also rich in protein, a good source of phosphorus, and a fair source of thiamine, riboflavin, vitamin C and iron.

1.2 kg (about 2½ lb) chicken, skinned, quartered and all excess fat removed
3 T ground coriander, dry-toasted until fragrant

5 T tamarind (*assam*), mixed with 2 C (500 ml) water and strained
2 T brown sugar
1½ T thick black soyasauce
½ tsp freshly ground black pepper

1. Marinate the chicken pieces in the rest of the ingredients for 8 hours, covered.

2. Heat a non-stick wok over moderate heat. Remove chicken pieces from marinade and pat completely dry. Fry the chicken pieces over low to moderate heat, turning often, until richly browned all over.

3. Add the marinade to the wok, bring to a boil, reduce the heat, and simmer until the chicken is tender, stirring occasionally, and basting with sauce. To serve, cut the chicken in smaller pieces, and moisten with the sauce.

Grilled Devilled Chicken

(serves 4-6)

	total	1 of 4 portions	1 of 6 portions
kcal	1332	333	222
fat (g)	55	14	9
sodium (mg)	986	247	164
dietary fibre (g)	7	2	1
cholesterol (mg)	765	191	128

This dish is quick, mildly spicy and delicious, as well as being a good source of protein and phosphorus, and a fair source of thiamine, riboflavin and iron.

1.2 kg (about 2½ lb) chicken, quartered (2 breasts with wings and 2 thighs with drumsticks)
1 red chilli, seeded and pounded
3 cloves garlic, pounded

3 tsp Dijon or whole-grain mustard
1 tsp soyasauce
1 tsp soya or olive oil
freshly ground black pepper
1 tsp fresh lime (or lemon) juice

1. *Remove skin from chicken breasts, legs and thighs — it will be impossible to completely remove skin from wings. Mix together pounded chilli, garlic, mustard, soyasauce and oil. Taste and add pepper and lime juice if desired.*

2. *Preheat an oven grill or charcoal grill. Brush chicken with the sauce from step 1, and let marinate 15 minutes. Then grill chicken, turning frequently, and basting with sauce until done, about 15-25 minutes.*

Variation: coat chicken with sauce, wrap in tinfoil and bake.

Reduced-Fat Beef Rendang

(serves 6-8)

	total	1 of 6 portions	1 of 8 portions
kcal	2176	363	272
fat (g)	103	17	13
sodium (mg)	1700	283	213
dietary fibre (g)	29	5	4
cholesterol (mg)	338	56	42

This Beef Rendang is considerably lower in fat and kilocalories than the classic dish. The original recipe has 658 kilocalories and 48 grams of fat per serving (based on 1 of 6 servings). This version weighs in at only 363 kilocalories and 17 grams of fat, with plenty of good taste. The low-kilocalorie version is also rich in protein, B vitamins, iron and zinc, with a fair amount of beta-carotene and vitamin C.

2 T soya oil
8 shallots, pounded
3 slices galingale (*lengkuas*), pounded
2.5 cm (1") piece fresh ginger, pounded
20 dried red chillies, soaked, seeded and pounded
2 stems lemon grass (*serai*), finely sliced and pounded
2 cloves garlic, pounded

6 T freshly grated coconut (substitute: 4 T dried, unsweetened coconut)
500 g (1 lb) tender beef (topside), cut into 5 cm (2") cubes
1 C (250 ml) thin coconut milk
¾ C (190 ml) evaporated milk mixed with 1½ C (375 ml) water
½ tsp salt
1 tsp sugar

1. Heat oil in a deep pot and fry pounded ingredients over moderate heat for 5 minutes. Meantime, in a non-stick pan, dry-fry the grated coconut until golden brown, stirring constantly. Add the coconut to the pounded mixture and fry for one minute. Add the beef and fry, stirring constantly until the beef loses its red colour.

2. Add the coconut milk, evaporated milk and water, salt and sugar, and stir constantly until the mixture boils. Reduce heat to low, and simmer until the beef is very tender and almost all the liquid has cooked away. Add a few T water if the dish looks too dry during the cooking process. If there is a visible layer of oil on the finished dish, skim and discard.

Bulgogi (Barbecued Beef Slices)

(serves 4-6)

	total	1 of 4 portions	1 of 6 portions
kcal	1047	262	175
fat (g)	59	15	10
sodium (mg)	1332	333	222
dietary fibre (g)	4	1	.7
cholesterol (mg)	295	74	49

This classic dish is rich in protein, iron, zinc and vitamin B complex.

500 g (1 lb) beef sirloin or tenderloin, very thinly sliced into 4 cm × 7 cm (1½" × 3") pieces
1 T light soyasauce

1 T garlic, minced
1 T sugar
½ T freshly ground black pepper
1 T sesame paste
1 T sesame oil

1. *Put beef slices in a bowl. In another bowl, combine soyasauce, garlic, sugar, pepper, and sesame paste; mix well and pour over beef. Toss to coat beef slices evenly. Add the sesame oil, and blend again. Cover and marinate in the refrigerator for 4 hours.*

2. *Heat a table-top barbecue or grill (or a cast-iron skillet or tawa) over moderately high heat. Wipe the surface of the grill with a few drops of soya oil to prevent meat from sticking, and grill until meat loses its red colour. Serve with Korean Crispy Pear Salad (see recipe page 156).*

Skewered Beef (Bo Lui)

(serves 6-8)

	total	1 of 6 portions	1 of 8 portions
kcal	1966	328	246
fat (g)	93	16	12
sodium (mg)	13,223	2204	1653
dietary fibre (g)	27	5	3
cholesterol (mg)	472	79	59

This dish is much lighter and more delicate than most skewered beef dishes. It's rich in protein, iron, zinc, thiamine, niacin, vitamins B6 and B12, biotin, pantothenic acid and folacin.

800 g (1¾ lb) beef fillet, sliced into .3 cm × 5 cm × 9 cm (⅛" × 2" × 3½") pieces
1 tsp garlic, pounded
2 T soya or corn oil
2 T soyasauce
6 T *nuoc-mam* sauce (see recipe page 41)
2 T lemon grass, pounded
1 tsp five spice powder
1 tsp sugar
½ tsp salt
½ tsp ground black pepper
200 g (7 oz) onion, peeled and sliced into 1.25 cm × 4 cm (½" × 1½") slivers
100 g (4 oz) bean sprouts, washed, trimmed and dried
12 skewers

Sauce:

1 tsp garlic, pounded
4 tsp fresh lemon juice
4 T lukewarm water
4 T *nuoc-mam* sauce (see recipe page 41)
12 pickled shallots, shredded

Garnish:

2 spring onions, cut into 5 cm (2") pieces, and ends cut into brushes
1 lemon, thinly sliced
1 cucumber, peeled and thinly sliced
1 small bunch of mint, washed and dried
1 small bunch of coriander, washed and dried
12 dark green lettuce leaves

1. *Marinate the beef slices in the garlic, oil, soyasauce,* nuoc-mam *sauce, lemon grass, five spice powder, sugar, salt and pepper for at least one hour.*

2. *On each slice of beef place some onion slivers and a few bean sprouts; roll up tightly. Thread about five beef rolls on each skewer while you heat a charcoal grill or oven grill.*

3. *Grill for 3-5 minutes on each side, depending on preference. Do 6 skewers at a time, to prevent crowding the grill. Mix sauce ingredients together and put into individual dishes. Remove beef from skewers at table; garnish with spring onions, lemon, cucumber, mint and coriander. Wrap in lettuce leaves before eating.*

Chilli con Carne

(serves 10-12)

	total	1 of 10 portions	1 of 12 portions
kcal	4679	468	390
fat (g)	123	12	10
sodium (mg)	3284	328	274
dietary fibre (g)	53	5	4
cholesterol (mg)	590	59	49

This excellent, one-pot Mexican meal is rich in protein, fibre, pantothenic acid, and vitamins B1, B6 and B12, a good source of zinc, vitamin C and beta-carotene, and a fair source of iron. It freezes well and you can make it as hot as you want by adding more or less cayenne. (The chilli will be much better if prepared a day ahead; most tomato-based dishes benefit from a day or so of "ripening.")

3 T olive oil
2 C onion, chopped
2 T garlic, minced
1 kg (2.2 lb) topside beef, minced
5 T Mexican chilli powder (available where imported spices are sold)
1 tsp dried oregano
1 T ground cumin
1 T ground chilli (cayenne)

3 C imported, tinned plum tomatoes, drained and chopped
2 C (500 ml) low-sodium, tinned beef stock
1 170 g (6 oz) tin tomato paste
3½ C freshly cooked red kidney beans
1 tsp salt
freshly ground black pepper

1. In a large, heavy saucepan, heat the olive oil over moderate heat. Add onions, and cook 7-8 minutes, until soft and golden. Stir in the garlic, and cook for another 2 minutes. Then add the beef, and stir until it loses its red colour.

2. Add the chilli powder, oregano, cumin and ground chilli, and stir to blend well. Then add the tomatoes, beef stock, tomato paste, kidney beans, salt and pepper. Bring to a boil, then partially cover the pot, and simmer for 1½ hours, stirring frequently.

VIETNAMESE

Fortune Rolls (Goi Cuon)

(yields 8 pieces)

	total	1 piece
kcal	753	94
fat (g)	24	3
sodium (mg)	2192	274
dietary fibre (g)	14	2
cholesterol (mg)	523	65

This dish is high in protein, iron, thiamine, niacin, vitamins B6 and B12, pantothenic acid, choline, folic acid and vitamin C, and a fair source of vitamin A. (Note: since Vietnamese rice leaves are not readily available, I've offered a version using spring roll wrappers.)

1 egg, lightly beaten
200 g (7 oz) very lean pork
2 T light soyasauce mixed with 2 T water
1 T five spice powder
8 pieces Vietnamese rice leaves (available at Thai specialty food shops) or substitute: 8 pieces prepared spring roll skins
8 local lettuce leaves
100 g (4 oz) bean sprouts, rinsed and thoroughly dried

1 cucumber (about 225 g or 8 oz), peeled, seeded and cut into .3 cm (⅛") strips
1 small bunch mint, washed, trimmed and tough stems removed
1 bunch coriander, washed and trimmed
1 small bunch chives
2 spring onions, quartered
8 medium prawns, cooked and halved lengthwise

1. *Heat a non-stick frying pan over moderate heat, and add the beaten egg. Swirl the pan around until the egg is set and dry, peel out the resulting thin omelette, cool, and cut into 6 cm (¼") strips.*

2. *Marinate the pork in the soyasauce, water and five spice powder for 30 minutes. Then grill until the meat completely loses its red colour, and slice into paper-thin slices.*

3. *On each of the rice leaves or spring roll wrappers, place a lettuce leaf, topped with equal portions of omelette strips, pork, bean sprouts, cucumber strips, mint, coriander, chives and spring onions; top with 2 prawn halves, and then roll into a tight cylinder, folding the ends in to enclose the filling. Garnish with additional mint and coriander sprigs, and serve immediately with dipping sauce (see next recipe). The rice leaves or spring roll wrappers tend to dry out if they sit too long.*

Variation: substitute 100 g (4 oz) cooked bee hoon for the bean sprouts.

Dipping Sauce

	total
kcal	223
fat (g)	15
sodium (mg)	3157
dietary fibre (g)	5
cholesterol (mg)	0

1 T hoisin sauce
3 T *nuoc-mam* sauce (see recipe below)
1 T roasted peanuts, crushed

1.   *Mix all ingredients together and serve with fortune rolls.*

VIETNAMESE

Nuoc-Mam Sauce

---

	total
kcal	385
fat (g)	6
sodium (mg)	32,073
dietary fibre (g)	14
cholesterol (mg)	0

The best *nuoc-mam* sauce comes from the island of Phu-Quoc in Vietnam. If it's not available, try this version.

---

2 large limes, peeled and seeded
5 cloves garlic
2 fresh red chillies, seeded and sliced
1 tsp vinegar

1 C (250 ml) water
1½ T sugar
2 C (500 ml) plain fish sauce

1.   *Pound together the lime pulp, garlic and chillies, and mix with the vinegar and water.*

2.   *Add the sugar and fish sauce, and leave to marinate for 24 hours. Strain the sauce and discard the garlic, chillies and lime. Nuoc-mam will keep for months.*

Pork Vindaloo

(serves 4-6)

	total	1 of 4 portions	1 of 6 portions
kcal	1809	452	302
fat (g)	96	24	16
sodium (mg)	1687	422	281
dietary fibre (g)	17	4	3
cholesterol (mg)	621	155	104

Rich in protein, thiamine and other B vitamins, this dish is excellent when served with brown rice or *chapatis* (see recipe page 114) and a green or deep yellow vegetable dish. The vinegar adds just enough tartness to cut the richness of the meat.

4 cloves garlic, pounded
2.5 cm (1") piece fresh ginger, pounded
2.5 cm (1") piece fresh turmeric, pounded (or
 ½ tsp ground turmeric)
1 tsp ground red pepper (cayenne)
¼ tsp ground aniseed
1½ T ground coriander
2 tsp ground cumin
¼ tsp dry mustard

2 T soya oil
100 g (4 oz or about 2) onions, chopped
900 g (about 1¾ lb) lean, boneless pork, cut
 into 5 cm (2") cubes
2 C (500 ml) boiling water
½ tsp salt
3 T vinegar
a pinch each of ground cloves, ground
 cinnamon, ground cardamom

1. Mix the garlic, ginger, turmeric, red pepper, aniseed, coriander, cumin and mustard with enough water (2-3 T) to make a paste. Heat the oil over moderate heat, and fry onion until soft. Add paste to the frying onion, and stir for 3 minutes.

2. Add the pork pieces, coating each well with spice paste, and reduce the heat to low. Fry slowly for 10 minutes, turning the pork once, and adding up to 2 T water if the porks sticks to the pan. Add the boiling water and salt; cover and simmer 1½ hours or until pork is tender. Skim off any visible fat, and stir in the vinegar, cloves, cinnamon and cardamom.

Fish and Shellfish

Fish and Shellfish

CHINESE

Steamed Fish with Black Beans and Chilli

(serves 4-6)

	total	1 of 4 portions	1 of 6 portions
kcal	928	232	155
fat (g)	27	7	5
sodium (mg)	1086	272	181
dietary fibre (g)	16	4	3
cholesterol (mg)	413	103	69

This simple method of preparation is one of the best ways to deal with delicate, less fatty fishes. The dish is an excellent, low-kilocalorie source of protein, B vitamins and beneficial fish oils.

1 whole, white-fleshed fish like sea bass, garoupa or flounder, (about 750 g or 1 ½ lb), gutted, gilled and scaled
4 slices ginger
2 spring onions, cut into 5 cm (2") pieces
1½ T peanut oil
1 tsp garlic, finely chopped
1 whole fresh red chilli, seeded and finely chopped

½ tsp ginger, finely chopped
2 tsp salted black beans, rinsed thoroughly, drained and chopped
1 T Chinese rice wine
½ tsp sesame oil
1 spring onion, chopped into fine rings
chopped coriander

1. *Wash and clean fish thoroughly. Place the ginger and spring onion on a plate large enough to hold the fish; fit comfortably in a steamer. Lay the fish on top, and steam for about 10 minutes.*

2. *Just before the fish is cooked, heat the peanut oil in a small saucepan over moderate heat. Add the chopped garlic, chilli and ginger, and stir until soft, but not brown. Add the chopped black beans, and stir for a minute. Add the wine, and once it sizzles, turn off the heat and stir in the sesame oil.*

3. *Drain fish and pour the entire contents of the pan over. Garnish with spring onion rings and chopped coriander.*

44

Tandoori Fish

(serves 6-8)

	total	1 of 6 portions	1 of 8 portions
kcal	1123	187	140
fat (g)	23	4	3
sodium (mg)	2332	389	292
dietary fibre (g)	14	2	2
cholesterol (mg)	497	83	62

This dish is an excellent source of protein, B vitamins and fish oil, and a fair source of vitamin C and beta-carotene. It is also low in fat and kilocalories. The yoghurt adds some calcium, and is suitable for those who are lactose intolerant.

900 g (1¾ lb) firm-fleshed fish fillet (like threadfin/*ikan kurau* and sole)
½ tsp salt
1 tsp lemon juice
2 cloves garlic
2.5 cm (1") piece ginger
2.5 cm (1") piece fresh turmeric

½ tsp saffron threads
4 dried chillies
1 tsp *garam masala*
½ C skim-milk or low-fat yoghurt
150 g (5 oz) tomatoes, finely sliced
1 lemon, finely sliced

1. Season the fillets with salt and lemon juice; let stand for 20 minutes.

2. Grind garlic, ginger, turmeric, saffron and chillies to a smooth paste. Add the garam masala *and skim-milk/yoghurt, and mix well.*

3. Put fish fillets in a shallow baking dish, and pour the yoghurt and spice mixture over. Marinate 2 hours in the refrigerator, then 2 hours at room temperature.

4. Heat oven to 205°C (400°F or Gas Regulo 8). Bake fish 20 minutes, until lightly browned and flesh flakes easily. (Important note: baking time will depend on the thickness of the fillet. As a rule of thumb, allow about 10 minutes per 2.5 cm or 1". Check fish frequently so it does not overcook.) Garnish with tomato and lemon slices.

Grilled Fish with Chillies

(serves 4-6)

	total	1 of 4 portions	1 of 6 portions
kcal	1406	352	234
fat (g)	52	13	9
sodium (mg)	2364	591	394
dietary fibre (g)	11	3	2
cholesterol (mg)	720	180	120

This dish is an excellent source of protein, B vitamins, beneficial fish oils, vitamin C and beta-carotene, and a good source of fibre. It is low in kilocalories and fat and packed with nutrition. Baking the chillies tames their heat to a pleasingly mild tang. Don't neglect them — they're full of vitamins!

900 g (about 1¾ lb) threadfin (*ikan kurau*), cut into 5 cm x 7 cm (2" x 3") pieces
½ tsp salt
1.25 cm (½") piece ginger, pounded
2 cloves garlic, pounded
1 T thick coconut milk
150 g (5 oz or 1 medium) onion, pounded
1 egg, beaten

1 tsp ground black pepper
1½ T soyabean or peanut oil
250 g (8 oz or about 2) ripe tomatoes, sliced into .5 cm (¼") rings
450 g (about 1 lb) green chillies, stems removed
1 15 cm (6") piece of banana leaf or tinfoil
1 T lemon juice

1.   Clean and scale fish and cut into pieces, then pat dry with paper towels. Combine salt, ginger, garlic, coconut milk, onion, egg, black pepper and oil, and pour mixture over the fish pieces. Marinate at room temperature for 30 minutes.

2.   Preheat the oven to 205°C (400°F or Gas Regulo 8). Place half the chillies over the bottom of a casserole, then top with the fish pieces and the marinade. Cover the fish with the tomato slices and remaining green chillies, and top with the banana leaf/tinfoil.

3.   Grill or bake for about 20 minutes, until fish flakes easily. Sprinkle the fish with the lemon juice and serve.

INDIAN

Baked Curried Fish

(serves 4-6)

	total	1 of 4 portions	1 of 6 portions
kcal	892	223	149
fat (g)	37	9	6
sodium (mg)	1778	445	296
dietary fibre (g)	45	11	8
cholesterol (mg)	248	62	41

This dish is low in kilocalories and fat, high in protein, beneficial fish oils and B vitamins.

450 g (about 1 lb) firm, white-fleshed fish fillet (like threadfin/*ikan kurau* or snapper/*ikan merah*)
½ tsp salt
2 tsp ground turmeric
1 T fresh lime juice
1 T black mustard seed

4 red chillies, seeded
1 T grated coconut
1 T soya oil
3 medium onions, finely sliced
1 T tomato puree
2 red chillies, sliced
1 T coriander leaves, chopped

1. *Wash and scale fish, and cut into 5 cm (2") pieces. Rub with salt and turmeric mixed to a paste with the lime juice.*

2. *Grind mustard seed, seeded red chillies and coconut. Set aside.*

3. *Preheat oven to 205°C (400°F or Gas Regulo 8). In a non-stick pan, heat oil and fry onion slices until brown. Remove pan from heat and stir in the ground mixture and the tomato puree. Pour the mixture over the fish pieces, and turn about to coat well.*

4. *Place the coated fish pieces in a casserole and sprinkle with sliced chillies. Bake about 20 minutes, and just before serving, garnish with chopped coriander.*

INDONESIAN

Fish in Sambal and Sweet Soyasauce

(serves 4-6)

	total	1 of 4 portions	1 of 6 portions
kcal	784	196	131
fat (g)	26	7	4
sodium (mg)	2356	589	393
dietary fibre (g)	3	.8	.5
cholesterol (mg)	0	0	0

This dish has everything going for it — super nutrition, ease of preparation and excellent taste. It's also an excellent source of protein, thiamine, niacin, vitamin B6, choline, pantothenic acid, vitamin B12 and folic acid, as well as being very low in kilocalories and fat.

650 g (1½ lb) whole seabass or carp
¼ tsp salt
1½ T soya oil
1.25 cm (½") piece ginger, minced
3 cloves garlic, minced
1.25 cm (½") piece galingale (*lengkuas*), minced

150 g (5 oz or about 1) onion, coarsely chopped
2 tsp *sambal ulek* (Indonesian chillies and spices)
1 bay leaf (*salam*)
1 T sweet soyasauce (*kicap manis*)
2 tsp tamarind (*assam*) mixed with 1½ T water and strained

1. *Rub fish with salt. Heat oil over moderate heat in a kuali or wok with a lid; add ginger and garlic and stir 30 seconds. Add galingale and onion, and fry until onion is golden brown. Add* sambal ulek, *bay leaf, and sweet soyasauce and stir. Add fish and reduce heat to low.*

2. *Baste fish with sauce, cover kuali, and cook over very low heat for 15-20 minutes, basting frequently. (If fish sticks, add a little water.) Add the tamarind during the last five minutes, and serve hot.*

INDONESIAN

Grilled Fish

(serves 4-6)

	total	1 of 4 portions	1 of 6 portions
kcal	882	221	147
fat (g)	27	7	5
sodium (mg)	2243	561	374
dietary fibre (g)	.1	.03	.02
cholesterol (mg)	0	0	0

Like Fish in Sambal and Sweet Soyasauce (see page 48), this dish is a nutritional super-star: it's low in kilocalories and fat and very nutritious.

1½ T soya oil
1 T sweet soyasauce
2 tsp *sambal ulek* (Indonesian chillies and spices)

2 T water
650-900 g (1½-1¾ lb) whole firm-fleshed fish, split lengthwise

1. Mix oil, *soyasauce*, sambal ulek *and water and bring to a boil in a small saucepan. Remove from heat.*

2. *Grill fish in the oven or over charcoal, turning frequently, and basting with the mixture from step one until done.*

Acar Fish (Pickled Fish)

(serves 4-6)

	total	1 of 4 portions	1 of 6 portions
kcal	995	249	166
fat (g)	30	8	5
sodium (mg)	1254	314	209
dietary fibre (g)	15	4	3
cholesterol (mg)	544	136	91

Pickled fish is an excellent source of protein, beneficial fish oils and B vitamins.

680 g (about 1½ lb) Spanish mackerel (*ikan tenggiri*), cut into 1.25 cm (½") steaks
¼ tsp salt
8 shallots, peeled and finely sliced
8 cloves garlic, peeled and finely sliced
7.5 cm (3") piece fresh turmeric, peeled and finely sliced
1 T soya oil
2 red chillies, seeded and shredded
½ C (125 ml) vinegar
3 tsp sugar

1. *Rub each fish steak with salt and set aside 20 minutes. Dry the slices of shallot, garlic and turmeric in a slow oven set at 100°C (200°F or Gas Regulo 1) for about 20 minutes, or leave in the sun for 2-3 hours. (Keep spices separate.)*

2. *Heat ½ T oil in a non-stick pan, add the fish steaks; fry both sides over moderate heat until browned. Drain fish steaks of all visible oil on paper towels and place the fish in one layer in a flat enamel pan; scatter the garlic, shallots and chillies over the steaks.*

3. *Clean the frying pan, heat the remaining ½ T oil, and add the turmeric; fry until the oil is yellow. Discard the turmeric, and add the vinegar and sugar. Bring to a boil, and pour over the fish steaks. Let the fish marinate at least 6 hours, preferably overnight, well covered.*

Ikan Assam Pedas (Fish Curry with Tamarind)

(serves 4-6)

	total	1 of 4 portions	1 of 6 portions
kcal	1369	342	228
fat (g)	43	11	7
sodium (mg)	1179	295	197
dietary fibre (g)	15	4	3
cholesterol (mg)	400	100	67

This dish is a superb alternative to high-fat, coconut-based curries. It is very low in fat and kilocalories, rich in protein, beneficial fish oils, vitamins B1, B6 and B12, pantothenic acid and folic acid, and a fair source of iron, vitamin C and beta-carotene.

12 dried red chillies, soaked until soft, and seeded
1.25 cm (½") piece fresh ginger
8 shallots
4 cloves garlic
1 tsp shrimp paste (*belacan*)
500 g (1 lb) Spanish mackerel (*ikan tenggiri*) steaks cut 1.8 cm (¾") thick

¼ tsp salt
½ tsp ground turmeric
2 T soya oil
200 g (7 oz or about 2) onions, finely sliced
½ C tamarind (*assam*) mixed with ¾ C (190 ml) water and strained
optional: ½ tsp palm sugar (*gula melaka* or substitute: brown sugar)

1. *Pound together: dried chillies, ginger, shallots, garlic and shrimp paste. Rinse and dry fish steaks; mix salt and turmeric, and rub over fish. Set aside for 5 minutes. Heat 1 T oil in a non-stick pan over moderate heat; add fish steaks and fry until golden brown on both sides. Remove and drain.*

2. *Place remaining 1 T oil in a kuali or wok and heat until moderately hot; add pounded ingredients and onions, and fry until onion is soft and golden. Begin adding a little of the tamarind liquid if mixture sticks to the pan. Then add the rest of the tamarind water and the fried fish and simmer until fish is tender; taste, and if necessary add the palm sugar. Do not overcook.*

INTERNATIONAL

Steamed Sole with Orange and Soyasauce
(serves 6)

	total	1 of 6 portions
kcal	801	134
fat (g)	20	3
sodium (mg)	1865	311
dietary fibre (g)	23	4
cholesterol (mg)	330	55

This dish is rich in protein, vitamins B1, B12 and B6, niacin, pantothenic acid and folic acid, and a good source of vitamin A. It is also very low in kilocalories and fat.

300 g (10 oz) snowpeas, washed and stringed
120 g (4 oz or about 3) carrots, scraped and cut into 2.5 cm × .6 cm (1" × ¼") sticks
⅛ tsp salt
white pepper
600 g (1¼ lb or 6 fillets) sole, cut in half lengthwise
12 very thin ginger slices
6 spring onions, each cut into 2 pieces 6 cm (2½") long

Sauce:

1 tsp sesame oil
1½ tsp soya oil
1 orange peel, white skin discarded, very finely shredded
1 tsp ginger, minced
1 tsp garlic, minced
2 tsp light soyasauce
1 T water

1. Arrange snowpeas and carrots in the bottom of a steamer. Sprinkle with salt and pepper.

2. Starting at the narrow end, roll up each piece of fish around a slice of ginger and a piece of spring onion. Arrange fish rolls on top of vegetables, and steam for about 8 minutes, or until fish is opaque and just done.

3. While fish steams, make the sauce: heat the sesame and soya oils over moderate heat, and stir in the orange peel. Cook 30 seconds and add the ginger and garlic; stir until fragrant, about 30 seconds, then stir in the soyasauce and water. Bring to a boil, and remove from heat. Serve with the fish and vegetables.

INDIAN

Prawn Curry with Yoghurt

(serves 6)

	total	1 of 6 portions
kcal	1612	269
fat (g)	41	7
sodium (mg)	2727	455
dietary fibre (g)	13	2
cholesterol (mg)	1813	302

When combined with *chapatis* or rice and a dark green or deep yellow vegetable, this dish makes a prudent, well-balanced meal. It's also rich in protein and vitamin C.

900 g (about 1¾ lb) large prawns in the shell
3 tsp ground turmeric
½ tsp salt
250 g (8 oz) medium potatoes, quartered
2 T soya oil
1 tsp cumin seed
2 sticks cinnamon
3 green cardamom pods, crushed

250 g (8 oz or about 3 medium) onions, finely sliced
1½ tsp ground chilli
1 T coriander powder
1 tsp ginger juice
1 tsp brown sugar or jaggery
2 C (500 ml) boiling water
¾ C skim-milk yoghurt
150 g (5 oz) ripe tomato, quartered

1. Shell, devein and rinse prawns. Coat prawns with 2 tsp turmeric and salt, and set aside for 30 minutes. Rub potatoes with 1 tsp turmeric.

2. Heat the oil over medium heat, and fry the cumin, cinnamon and cardamom for one minute. Add the sliced onions and potatoes, and fry for another 5 minutes. Then add ground chilli, coriander powder, ginger juice, and sugar. Mix well and add boiling water. Simmer until the sauce is thickened and the potatoes are tender, but not overdone. Add prawns and yoghurt, and simmer an additional 3-5 minutes until the prawns are just done. Just before serving, add the quartered tomato.

Sambal Udang (Prawns with Chilli)

(serves 4-6)

	total	1 of 4 portions	1 of 6 portions
kcal	981	245	164
fat (g)	31	8	5
sodium (mg)	1073	268	179
dietary fibre (g)	19	5	3
cholesterol (mg)	1000	250	167

This dish is rich in protein, and a good source of B vitamins, trace minerals and calcium.

15 dried red chillies, soaked and seeded
10 shallots
4 cloves garlic
1.25 cm (½") piece ginger
1 tsp shrimp paste (*belacan*)
1½ T soya oil

150 g (5 oz or about 1 medium) onion, finely sliced
500 g (1 lb) prawns, peeled and cleaned
85 g (3 oz or about 1) tomato, quartered
1 tsp sugar
2 T tamarind (*assam*) mixed with ½ C (125 ml) water and strained

1. Pound together: chillies, shallots, garlic, ginger and shrimp paste. Heat oil in a kuali or wok and add pounded ingredients and onion slices. Fry over moderate heat for 4 minutes, until onions are softened and the ground ingredients are fragrant.

2. Add prawns and fry for 1 minute, until they begin to turn pink; add the tomato, sugar and tamarind, and simmer gently until the prawns are just done.

VIETNAMESE

Prawn on Sugar Cane (Chao Tom)

(serves 8)

	total	1 of 8 portions
kcal	1165	146
fat (g)	9	1
sodium (mg)	6806	851
dietary fibre (g)	66	8
cholesterol (mg)	1000	125

The restaurant version of this dish is often deep-fried (rather than poached and grilled), which adds unnecessary fat and kilocalories. This version is rich in protein, iron, iodine, copper and zinc, as well as being lower in fat and kilocalories.

500 g (1 lb) large prawns, shelled and cleaned
1 clove garlic, pounded
½ tsp salt
½ tsp ground black pepper
20 g (¾ oz) baking powder
8 sticks sugar cane, cut into 10 cm (4")
  lengths
100 g (4 oz) onion, coarsely chopped
4 T potato flour (substitute: rice flour or corn
  flour)

Sauce:

40 g (1½ oz) garlic, pounded
4 T vinegar
4 T lukewarm water
4 T *nuoc-mam* sauce (see recipe page 41)

Garnish:

8 dark green lettuce leaves
mint sprigs
coriander sprigs

1. Marinate the prawns in the garlic, salt, pepper and baking powder; let sit one hour.

2. Peel sugar cane pieces, rinse and thoroughly dry.

3. Puree the onion and the potato flour with the prawn mixture in a blender or food processor, and divide the mixture into 8 portions. Shape each portion around the centre of each sugar cane piece, leaving about an inch of sugar cane free at each end (for picking up).

4. Plunge the wrapped sugar cane into a deep pan of boiling water, and then simmer over moderate heat for 15 minutes. Drain thoroughly while you heat a charcoal grill or an oven grill.

5. Grill or broil for 5 minutes, until lightly golden. Mix sauce ingredients together and put into individual dishes. Serve with sauce and garnish with lettuce leaves, mint and coriander sprigs.

MALAY

Stuffed Squid with Chilli

(serves 4-6)

	total	1 of 4 portions	1 of 6 portions
kcal	1844	461	307
fat (g)	40	10	7
sodium (mg)	2610	653	435
dietary fibre (g)	9	2	2
cholesterol (mg)	890	223	148

This dish is protein-rich, and a good source of B vitamins and trace minerals.

Stuffing:

8 medium squids, skinned and cleaned
2 tsp soya oil
2 dried chillies, soaked until soft, seeded and pounded
4 shallots, pounded
1 clove garlic, pounded
125 g (4 oz) prawns, shelled, cleaned and coarsely chopped
sharp toothpicks

Sauce:

1 T soya oil
1 tsp shrimp paste (*belacan*), pounded
6 dried chillies, soaked, seeded and pounded
8 shallots, peeled and pounded
.6 cm (¼") piece galingale (*lengkuas*), pounded
2 cloves garlic
1 stem lemon grass (*serai*), bruised
½ C tamarind (*assam*) mixed with 1¼ C (315 ml) water and strained

1. *Set the cleaned squids and their heads aside. To make the stuffing: heat the 2 tsp oil over moderate heat and fry the 2 chillies, 4 shallots and garlic clove for 1 minute; add the prawns and fry gently for 3 minutes. Remove from heat and cool. Stuff the body cavities of each squid with the fried prawn mixture, set the heads back in place, and secure with toothpicks.*

2. *To make the sauce: heat the 1 T oil over moderate heat and add the pounded shrimp paste, 6 chillies, 8 shallots, galingale and 2 cloves garlic; fry for 4 minutes, and add the lemon grass and tamarind water. Add the stuffed squid and simmer gently for about 5 minutes, until the squid is cooked through, but not tough.*

Mussels in Soyabean Sauce and Chilli, page 58

Reduced-Fat Bean Curd with Chilli (Ma Po Tofu), page 60, and Fried Bean Curd and Spring Onions, page 61

MALAY

Sambal Sotong (Chilli Squids)

(serves 4-6)

	total	1 of 4 portions	1 of 6 portions
kcal	1460	365	243
fat (g)	31	8	5
sodium (mg)	3060	765	510
dietary fibre (g)	15	4	3
cholesterol (mg)	250	63	42

This nutritious dish is light in kilocalories and fat, rich in protein, a good source of vitamin C, and a fair source of beta-carotene.

500 g (1 lb) large squids, cleaned and skinned, heads and long tentacles cut in half, bodies cut into 1.8 cm (¾") rings
2 tsp shrimp paste (*belacan*)
12 dried chillies, soaked until soft, seeded
10 shallots
3 cloves garlic
1½ T soya oil

200 g (7 oz or about 2) onions, cut into .6 cm (¼") rings
1 stem lemon grass (*serai*), bruised
2 T water
4 T tamarind (*assam*) mixed with 8 T water and strained
2 tsp palm sugar (*gula melaka* or substitute: brown sugar)

1. *Set the squid aside while making the* rempah: *pound together the shrimp paste, chillies, shallots and garlic. Heat the oil in a kuali or wok over moderately high heat; add the onion rings and fry until soft. Add the pounded ingredients and lemon grass and fry 4 minutes, adding 2 T water if the mixture sticks to the pan.*

2. *Add the tamarind and palm sugar, and bring to a boil. Reduce the heat to moderate, and add the squids. Stirring frequently, cook for 2-3 minutes, until just done. Don't overcook — the squid toughens easily.*

Mussels in Soyabean Sauce and Chilli

(serves 4-6)

	total	1 of 4 portions	1 of 6 portions
kcal	433	108	72
fat (g)	21	5	4
sodium (mg)	745	186	124
dietary fibre (g)	15	4	3
cholesterol (mg)	240	60	40

Health experts recommend eating *all* shellfish cooked beyond the usual "until the shells open" stage. To inactivate any bacteria and viruses, the shellfish needs to get quite hot inside. In this recipe, once the mussels are open they get an additional steaming. Mussels are a good source of calcium, and phosphorus, and a fair source of iron. They are also naturally salty — so cut down on the *taucheo* if the dish is too salty for your taste.

600 g (1¼ lb) mussels in the shells
1 T soyabean oil
3 cloves garlic, minced
3 shallots, minced

1½ tsp preserved soyabeans (*taucheo*),
  rinsed and pounded to a paste
5 cm (2") piece ginger, shredded
2 red chillies, seeded and cut into fine rings
½ tsp sugar

1. Scrub mussels clean; press the shells of each one together, and discard any which remain open after pressing. Soak clean mussels in a large bowl of water for one hour.

2. Heat the oil in a wok over moderate heat, and fry the garlic and shallots until soft. Add the soyabean paste and stir over low to moderate heat for 3 minutes. Add ginger, chillies and mussels and stir-fry over high heat for 1 minute. Add sugar and continue stirring until all the mussels open — discard any that do not open. Cover the wok, and cook over moderate heat for 1 minute, then serve in deep bowls.

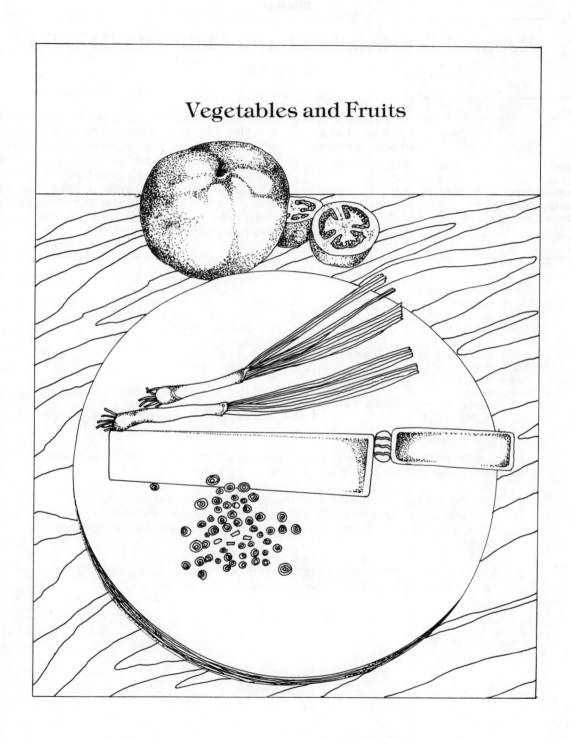

Vegetables and Fruits

CHINESE

Reduced-Fat Bean Curd with Chilli (Ma Po Tofu)

(serves 4-6)

	total	1 of 4 portions	1 of 6 portions
kcal	995	249	166
fat (g)	43	11	7
sodium (mg)	3562	891	594
dietary fibre (g)	6	2	1
cholesterol (mg)	89	22	15

This is an inexpensive dish that is rich in protein, iron and calcium. The small amount of meat stretches the vegetable protein in the *tofu*, and adds B vitamins. Although the dish is low in kilocalories and relatively low in fat, it's quite substantial. Add a light, salt-free soup, a small bowl of rice, and a portion of deep green or yellow-orange vegetable, and you have a well-balanced meal.

4 soft soyabean curd squares (*tofu*)
1 T soyabean oil
½ T sesame oil
4 shallots, pounded
4 cloves garlic, pounded
1.25 cm (½") piece ginger, pounded
150 g (5 oz) lean beef, minced
1 T preserved soyabeans (*taucheo*), rinsed
  and pounded
4 spring onions, washed, trimmed, and cut
  into 5 cm (2") pieces

2 tsp light soyasauce
1 tsp ground Sichuan peppercorns or ½ tsp
  ground black pepper
1 T Chinese rice wine
1 T tomato puree
2 T tomato ketchup
2½ tsp ground red chilli
1 T dark soyasauce
½ C (125 ml) salt-free chicken stock (see
  recipe page 140)
1 T cornflour mixed with 3 T chicken stock

1. *Dice the bean curd into 1.5 cm (¾") cubes, place in a colander in the sink, and allow water to drain off for 30 minutes.*

2. *Heat the oils in a wok or kuali over moderate heat; add the pounded shallots, garlic and ginger, and fry for 30 seconds. Then add the minced beef and fry until it loses its pink colour. Add the preserved soyabeans and spring onions and stir.*

3. *Add remaining ingredients except the cornflour paste and bring to a boil; add the cornflour paste and stir-fry until the sauce is thickened and clear.*

CHINESE

Fried Bean Curd and Spring Onions
(serves 4-6)

	total	1 of 4 portions	1 of 6 portions
kcal	257	64	43
fat (g)	20	5	3
sodium (mg)	879	220	147
dietary fibre (g)	2	.5	.3
cholesterol (mg)	0	0	0

This is another simple yet marvelously satisfying dish that's easy on the heart and waistline. It's very low in kilocalories and fat, and rich in protein, calcium and iron.

1 T soya oil
1.25 cm (½") piece ginger, very thinly sliced
3 pieces firm soyabean cake (*taukwa*), dried and cut into 1.25 cm (½") squares

20 spring onions, trimmed and cut into 2.5 cm (1") pieces
1 T light soyasauce

1. Heat the oil over moderately high heat and add the ginger slices. Stir for 10 seconds and add the bean curd squares. Cook, stirring occasionally, until the bean curd is crisp and golden. Stir in the spring onions and cook for 2 minutes over moderate heat, stirring occasionally. Add soyasauce, stir thoroughly and serve.

MALAY

Reduced-Fat Tempe Goreng

(serves 4-6)

	total	1 of 4 portions	1 of 6 portions
kcal	1168	292	195
fat (g)	45	11	8
sodium (mg)	1220	305	203
dietary fibre (g)	6	2	1
cholesterol (mg)	0	0	0

Tempe is a very inexpensive source of high-quality vegetable protein that can make an important contribution to diet. All too often though, it is fried in a great deal of oil, which makes it rich in fat and kilocalories. In this version very little oil is used. The result is much lower in kilocalories and fat, rich in protein, and a fair source of calcium, iron and phosphorus.

6 fermented soyabean cakes (*tempe*)
2 tsp tamarind (*assam*) mixed with 1 T water and strained

1½ tsp ground turmeric
½ tsp salt
1 T soya oil

1. *Rub the fermented soyabean cakes with tamarind mixed with turmeric and salt; let stand 30 minutes.*

2. *Heat oil a teaspoon at a time in a non-stick pan; when very hot, add half the* tempe, *and fry, pressing down with the back of a spatula to hasten browning. Keep turning to brown evenly. Add a few more drops of oil if needed, and cover the pan occasionally to hasten cooking. Use the remaining oil to fry the rest of the* tempe. *Cut each cake into 5 cm (2") square pieces. Serve with* lontong *(see recipe page 92) or as a side dish.*

JAPANESE

Dengaku Tofu (Grilled Tofu with Sweet Soyabean Paste)

(serves 4-6)

	total	1 of 4 portions	1 of 6 portions
kcal	306	77	51
fat (g)	14	4	2
sodium (mg)	27	7	5
dietary fibre (g)	26	7	4
cholesterol (mg)	0	0	0

This tofu dish is a good source of protein and a fair source of calcium.

2 pieces Japanese *tofu*, cut into 2 cm x 7.5
cm (¾" × 3") pieces (yields 8 pieces)
15 g (1 oz) spinach, dropped into boiling water
for 2 minutes, drained and pounded to a
paste

115 g (4 oz) *shiro miso* (white soyabean
paste)
kona sansho (Japanese pepper condiment)

1. *Preheat the oven grill to its highest point. Put* tofu *pieces in a snugly fitting flameproof dish, add enough water to reach halfway up the sides of the* tofu *pieces, and broil until* tofu *is speckled with brown. Turn, and broil the other side. Set aside.*

2. *Mix the pounded spinach with half the* shiro miso *and a dash of* kona sansho. *Spread half the* tofu *pieces with this mixture, and half with plain* miso. *Use a fork to make lines in the* miso *topping. Skewer each piece of* tofu *with two flat skewers, return the* tofu *to the pan of water, and broil under high heat until the* miso *topping is slightly browned.*

SINGAPOREAN

Fried Leeks

(serves 4-6)

	total	1 of 4 portions	1 of 6 portions
kcal	357	89	60
fat (g)	17	4	3
sodium (mg)	775	194	129
dietary fibre (g)	26	7	4
cholesterol (mg)	0	0	0

This dish is a good foil to rich or oily dishes, an excellent source of beta-carotene and dietary fibre, and a good source of vitamin C. The leeks must be perfectly dry and cooked quickly to preserve their crunchiness.

½ T soyabean oil
½ T sesame oil
400 g (14 oz or about 2 whole) leeks,
trimmed, thoroughly washed, dried and
finely sliced on the diagonal
3 shallots, finely sliced
2 red chillies, seeded and finely sliced

2 cloves garlic, finely sliced
1 tsp light soyasauce
1 tsp fish sauce
1 tsp sugar
1 T light rice vinegar
juice of 1 lime

1. *Heat oils over moderately high heat. Add sliced leeks, shallots, chillies and garlic, and stir-fry for 3 minutes, until the leeks are crisp but tender.*

2. *Add the soyasauce, fish sauce, sugar and vinegar, and cook briskly until the liquid is evaporated. Serve with lime juice sprinkled over the top.*

SINGAPOREAN

Fried Bean Sprouts

(serves 4-6)

	total	1 of 4 portions	1 of 6 portions
kcal	300	75	50
fat (g)	21	5	4
sodium (mg)	11	3	2
dietary fibre (g)	21	5	4
cholesterol (mg)	0	0	0

This dish is simple and delicious as well as an excellent source of vitamin C and a fair source of beta-carotene.

½ T soyabean oil
½ T sesame oil
4 cloves garlic, minced
2 red chillies, seeded and finely sliced

300 g (10 oz) bean sprouts, washed and
  thoroughly drained
½ tsp black pepper
1 tsp fish sauce

1. *Heat the oils over moderately high heat; add the garlic and chillies and stir for 30 seconds. Add the bean sprouts, and stir-fry for 1-2 minutes, until hot, but very crisp.*

2. *Add the black pepper and fish sauce, toss together well and serve.*

CHINESE

Baby Corn with Snowpeas

(serves 4-6)

	total	1 of 4 portions	1 of 6 portions
kcal	454	114	76
fat (g)	23	6	4
sodium (mg)	4941	1235	824
dietary fibre (g)	150	38	25
cholesterol (mg)	0	0	0

This delicate, naturally sweet dish is rich in dietary fibre, and low in kilocalories and fat. It goes particularly well with bland, low-texture fish dishes.

350 g (12 oz) baby corn
1½ T soyabean oil
4 cloves garlic, minced
250 g (8 oz) snowpeas, washed and stringed
1 tsp light soyasauce

2 T rice wine
1 tsp sugar
¼ tsp salt
½ C (125 ml) blanching liquid from baby corn
   (or use ½ C plain water)
1 tsp cornflour mixed with 2 tsp cold water

1. *If using fresh baby corn: trim each ear and blanch in boiling water for 3 minutes. Drain, reserving ½ C of the blanching liquid, and slice each ear in half lengthwise. If using tinned baby corn: drain, rinse thoroughly and slice each ear in half lengthwise.*

2. *Heat the oil over moderately high heat; add the garlic and stir for 30 seconds. Add the snowpeas and stir-fry for 2 minutes. Add corn and stir. Add remaining ingredients except cornflour paste and bring to a boil. Add cornflour paste and stir until sauce is thickened and clear. Serve.*

CHINESE

Stir-Fried Snowpeas with Bamboo Shoots and Mushrooms

(serves 4-6)

	total	1 of 4 portions	1 of 6 portions
kcal	467	117	78
fat (g)	23	6	4
sodium (mg)	1025	256	171
dietary fibre (g)	30	8	5
cholesterol (mg)	0	0	0

This dish is delightfully crispy, quick and easy to prepare. It's also rich in dietary fibre, vitamin C, thiamine, niacin, phosphorus and riboflavin.

1½ T soyabean oil
6 dried Chinese mushrooms, soaked in warm
   water until soft, stemmed and cut into
   quarters
½ C tinned bamboo shoots, thinly sliced and
   cut into triangles

400 g (14 oz) snowpeas, washed and stringed
½ tsp salt
½ tsp sugar
2 T mushroom soaking liquid

1. *Heat the oil over moderately high heat, add the mushrooms and bamboo shoots and stir-fry for 2 minutes. Add the snowpeas, salt and sugar, and the mushroom soaking liquid. Cook, stirring constantly, for 2 minutes, until liquid evaporates. Serve.*

CHINESE

Broccoli with Dried Mushrooms
(serves 4-6)

	total	1 of 4 portions	1 of 6 portions
kcal	528	132	88
fat (g)	23	6	4
sodium (mg)	1598	400	266
dietary fibre (g)	22	6	4
cholesterol (mg)	0	0	0

This dish is an excellent source of dietary fibre, and a good source of beta-carotene, vitamin C, thiamine, riboflavin, niacin and phosphorus. Because of its richness, it is a good accompaniment to a light or bland fish or poultry dish. (Tip: save the broccoli stems for a salad. Peel and trim stems, cut into slices and blanch in boiling water for 3 minutes. Drain, cool and combine with ½ tsp each sesame oil, rice vinegar and light soyasauce.)

1½ T soyabean oil
350 g (12 oz) broccoli flowerets, blanched in boiling water for 2 minutes, drained and dried
8 large Chinese dried mushrooms, soaked in warm water until soft, stemmed, drained and cut into quarters

2 tsp light soyasauce
2 tsp rice wine
½ tsp sugar
2 tsp oyster sauce
½ C (125 ml) mushroom soaking liquid
1 T cornflour mixed with 2 T cold water

1. *Heat the oil over moderately high heat; add the broccoli and stir-fry 1 minute. Add the mushrooms and stir. Add all remaining ingredients except cornflour paste, and bring to a boil.*

2. *Add cornflour paste and stir until sauce is thickened and clear. Serve.*

INTERNATIONAL

Steamed Broccoli with Garlic and Lemon
(serves 6-8)

	total	1 of 6 portions	1 of 8 portions
kcal	308	51	39
fat (g)	15	3	2
sodium (mg)	560	93	70
dietary fibre (g)	17	3	2
cholesterol (mg)	0	0	0

This Italian dish is an excellent source of beta-carotene and vitamin C, a fair source of dietary fibre, and low in kilocalories and fat.

450 g (15 oz or about 1 bunch) broccoli,
  trimmed and broken into flowerets, (stems
  should be no longer than 5 cm or 2")
3 cloves garlic, minced

1 T olive oil
2 T fresh lemon juice
freshly ground black pepper
¼ tsp salt

1. *Steam the broccoli for about 7 minutes, until just done. Meantime, mix the garlic, olive oil, lemon juice, pepper and salt and blend well. When the broccoli is done, pour the sauce over and toss. Serve hot or at room temperature.*

INTERNATIONAL

Marinated Mushrooms

(yields 2 cups or 10 servings as an appetiser)

	total	1 of 10 servings
kcal	500	50
fat (g)	36	4
sodium (mg)	549	55
dietary fibre (g)	13	1
cholesterol (mg)	0	0

These mushrooms make a delicious part of an Italian cold dish and are a good source of fibre, phosphorus, thiamine, riboflavin and niacin. Allow the oil to drain off completely before serving.

½ C (125 ml) olive oil (extra virgin olive oil is
  preferable)
½ C (125 ml) water
juice of 2 large lemons
1 bay leaf

4 cloves garlic, smashed
6 whole black peppercorns
½ tsp salt
500 g (1 lb) fresh, small button mushrooms,
  trimmed and wiped clean

1. *Combine the olive oil, water, lemon juice, bay leaf, garlic, peppercorns, and salt in a stainless steel or enamelled skillet, and bring to a boil over high heat. Reduce the heat to low, cover and simmer for 15 minutes.*

2. *Drop mushrooms into the simmering marinade and cook uncovered, turning them over occasionally, for 5 minutes. Turn off the heat, and allow the mushrooms to cool in the marinade. When ready to serve, lift mushrooms out of marinade, drain, and dry. They are excellent as an appetiser, or sliced and added to salads or pizza toppings. (They will keep in the refrigerator for 2-3 days.)*

INDIAN

Carrot Pachadi

(serves 4-6)

	total	1 of 4 portions	1 of 6 portions
kcal	364	91	61
fat (g)	18	5	3
sodium (mg)	276	69	46
dietary fibre (g)	12	3	2
cholesterol (mg)	8	2	1

Use this dish as a side dish to boost nutrition — particularly in vegetarian meals. It is a rich source of beta-carotene, and a fair source of protein, fibre, calcium and B vitamins. And, it goes well with *chapatis* and *thosai* (see recipes pages 114 and 112).

250 g (8 oz) carrots, grated
6 shallots, finely sliced
5 g fresh red chilli (about ½ a chilli), sliced
2 tsp soya oil

2 tsp mustard seeds
1 dried red chilli, sliced in 2.5 cm (1") lengths
½ C plain, skim-milk yoghurt

1. Mix together carrots, shallots and red chilli. Heat oil over moderate heat and add mustard seeds and dried chilli. Stir for a minute and add the carrot mixture. Stir constantly for another minute, then remove to a bowl. Cool thoroughly and blend in yoghurt.

JAPANESE

Takeuchi String Beans with Peanut Sauce

(serves 4-6)

	total	1 of 4 portions	1 of 6 portions
kcal	255	64	43
fat (g)	12	3	2
sodium (mg)	1431	358	239
dietary fibre (g)	18	5	3
cholesterol (mg)	0	0	0

This remarkably simple, remarkably good home-style Japanese dish is a fair source of fibre, vitamin C, beta-carotene and protein.

2 C (500 ml) water
450 g (15 oz) string beans, washed, stringed,
    and trimmed
3 tsp light soyasauce

3-4 T smooth or chunky peanut butter,
    depending on preference
2 tsp black or white sesame seeds

1. *Place water in a kuali or wok with a cover. Bring to a boil, add string beans, reduce heat, cover and simmer until beans are just done.*

2. *Drain off all but 5 T water, then add the soyasauce and peanut butter and blend into a creamy sauce to completely coat the beans. (Add more or less peanut butter and/or water to taste). Garnish with black or white sesame seeds.*

NONYA

Sweet Potato Leaves in Sour Sauce

(serves 4-6)

	total	1 of 4 portions	1 of 6 portions
kcal	1269	317	212
fat (g)	46	12	8
sodium (mg)	340	85	57
dietary fibre (g)	57	14	10
cholesterol (mg)	28	7	5

This reduced-fat, reduced-kilocalorie version of a popular home-style dish is rich in vitamin C and beta-carotene and a good source of dietary fibre. The original recipe has 628 kilocalories and 37 grams of fat (based on 1 of 4 servings), while this version has only 317 kilocalories and 12 grams of fat.

450 g (about 1 lb) sweet potato leaves,
    washed, stems peeled and cut into 6.5 cm
    (2½") lengths
400 g (14 oz) sweet potato, peeled and cut
    into 2.5 cm (1") cubes
1 tsp dried prawns, soaked and pounded
3 red chillies, seeded and pounded

4 shallots, pounded
2 cloves garlic, pounded
1 tsp shrimp paste (*belacan*), pounded
1½ T soya oil
4 T tamarind (*assam*) mixed with 1 C (250 ml)
    water and strained
5 T thin coconut milk

1. *Set the sweet potato leaves and sweet potato cubes aside; fry the pounded ingredients in the oil over moderate heat for 3-4 minutes. Add the sweet potato cubes and sweet potato leaves, stir, and add the tamarind water. Bring to a boil, reduce the heat to low, cover and simmer 10-15 minutes, until vegetables are tender.*

2. *Add the thin coconut milk and simmer until the sauce is slightly thickened.*

INDONESIAN

Brinjal with Chilli (Sambal Goreng Terung)

(serves 4-6)

	total	1 of 4 portions	1 of 6 portions
kcal	391	98	65
fat (g)	16	4	3
sodium (mg)	1149	287	192
dietary fibre (g)	32	8	5
cholesterol (mg)	0	0	0

This dish is a good source of vitamin C and dietary fibre, as well as being very low in kilocalories and fat. Use small, firm brinjal for best results.

1 T tamarind (*assam*) mixed with 2 T water and strained
½ tsp salt
2 small (about 400 g or 14 oz) brinjal (eggplant/aubergine), thinly sliced
100 g (4 oz or about 1) onion, thinly sliced

1 T soya oil
1 tsp ground coriander
½ tsp palm sugar (*gula melaka*), (substitute: brown sugar)
40 g (1½ oz or about 4) red chillies, pounded
½ T shrimp paste (*belacan*), pounded
1 T water

1. Add tamarind mixed with salt to brinjal. Fry onion in oil over moderate heat until golden brown; add coriander, palm sugar and pounded chillies. Fry for 1 minute, add the shrimp paste, and fry 1 minute more.

2. Add brinjal and water (add more if necessary, 1 T at a time, as needed) and fry for 10 minutes, until brinjal is tender.

MALAY

Fried Water Convolvulus (Kangkong Tumis Belacan)

(serves 4-6)

	total	1 of 4 portions	1 of 6 portions
kcal	327	82	55
fat (g)	17	4	3
sodium (mg)	220	55	37
dietary fibre (g)	33	8	6
cholesterol (mg)	0	0	0

Kangkong is one of the most nutrient-dense vegetables there is. This recipe is low-fat, low-kilocalorie and very rich in beta-carotene, vitamins C, B1 and B2, folic acid, calcium, iron and dietary fibre.

1 tsp shrimp paste (*belacan*), toasted and
  pounded
½ tsp sugar
½ C (125 ml) water
1 T soya oil
100 g (4 oz or about 1) onion, finely sliced

4 cloves garlic, pounded
3 red chillies, seeded and sliced
400 g (14 oz) water convolvulus (*kangkong*),
  stalks cut into 2.5 cm (1") lengths, tough
  parts removed

1. *Thoroughly mix shrimp paste with sugar and water. Heat oil over moderate heat and fry the onion, garlic and chillies until the onion is soft, about 3 minutes. Add the shrimp paste mixture and the water convolvulus; cover the pan, and cook briskly for 5 minutes, or until the stems are tender and the leaves wilted.*

INDIAN

Spiced Potatoes with Mustard Seed

(serves 4-6)

	total	1 of 4 portions	1 of 6 portions
kcal	754	189	126
fat (g)	31	8	5
sodium (mg)	1032	258	172
dietary fibre (g)	13	3	2
cholesterol (mg)	0	0	0

This dish is an excellent source of carbohydrate, a good source of vitamin C and vitamin B6, and a fair source of fibre. It also makes a wonderful filling for *thosai* (see recipe page 112).

500 g (about 1 lb) medium potatoes,
  scrubbed but not peeled
2 T soya oil
¾ tsp mustard seeds
150 g (5 oz or 1 medium) onion, finely
  chopped

½ tsp salt
½ tsp ground turmeric
1 tsp ground chilli (cayenne)
¼ tsp ground black pepper

1. *Boil potatoes until just done. Drain, cool and dice into 1.25 cm (½") cubes. In a karhai, kuali or wok, heat oil over moderate heat and add mustard seeds. When seeds pop, add onion and salt, and fry for 7 minutes, until onion is golden brown.*

2. *Add turmeric, ground chilli and black pepper, and stir well. Add the diced potatoes and fry for 3 minutes, until potatoes are well coated and heated through. Serve as a filling for thosai, or as a vegetable side dish.*

INDIAN

Braised Cabbage

(serves 4-6)

	total	1 of 4 portions	1 of 6 portions
kcal	426	107	71
fat (g)	25	6	4
sodium (mg)	1032	258	172
dietary fibre (g)	20	5	3
cholesterol (mg)	0	0	0

This dish is an excellent source of beta-carotene and vitamin C and a good source of dietary fibre.

1½ T soya oil
1 tsp mustard seeds
20 g (¾ oz or about 2) green chillies, finely sliced
6 shallots, shredded (substitute: red onion)
2 sprigs curry leaves (*karuvapillai*)

1½ tsp black gram dhal (*urad dhal*)
500 g (1 lb) white cabbage, coarsely shredded
½ tsp sugar
½ tsp salt
4 T water

1. Heat oil over moderate heat in a karhai, kuali or wok; add mustard seeds and when they pop stir in chillies, shallots/red onions, curry leaves and black gram dhal. Fry 3 minutes, stirring constantly. Add cabbage and continue to fry for 1 minute.

2. Add sugar, salt and water, and cover. Simmer about 10 minutes, until cabbage is soft. Remove lid and cook briskly to evaporate any remaining water. Serve at room temperature.

Tandoori Chicken, page 21, and Saffron Brown Rice Pillau, page 91

Fried Bean Sprouts, page 64, Broccoli with Dried Mushrooms, page 66, and Stir-Fried Snowpeas with Bamboo Shoots and Mushrooms, page 65

Kimchee (Pickled Cabbage with Chilli)

(serves 8-10)

	total	1 of 8 portions	1 of 10 portions
kcal	336	42	34
fat (g)	6	.8	.6
sodium (mg)	2734	342	273
dietary fibre (g)	20	3	2
cholesterol (mg)	0	0	0

This home-made version of *kimchee* is far superior to what's available in the shops — and it's simple and fun to make.

900 g (1¾ lb or 1 whole) Chinese cabbage, sliced crosswise into 3 cm × 5 cm (1¼" × 2") pieces
1 T salt
1 T glutinous rice flour, mixed with 6 T water
4 spring onions, cut into 5 cm (2") pieces
30 g (1 oz) chives, cut into 5 cm (2") pieces

5 cloves garlic, minced
1.25 cm (½") piece ginger, minced
1 whole Korean crispy pear, peeled and thinly sliced into 3 cm × 5 cm (1¼" × 2") pieces
1 T sesame seeds, toasted
2 T red chilli paste
1½ T fish sauce

1. *Soak cabbage pieces in water to cover, mixed with salt. Let soak for 4 hours. Drain, rinse thoroughly, and drain again.*

2. *Put the glutinous rice flour and water mixture in a small saucepan; cook over moderate heat, until mixture becomes a paste. Pour into a small bowl, and add the spring onion, chives, garlic, ginger, crispy pear, toasted sesame seeds, red chilli paste and fish sauce. Add to the drained cabbage, mix well and place in an airtight container. Allow to ferment at room temperature for about 2 days (until well fermented), then refrigerate.*

INDIAN

Channa Dhal Curry

(serves 6-8)

	total	1 of 6 portions	1 of 8 portions
kcal	1698	283	212
fat (g)	51	9	6
sodium (mg)	1040	173	130
dietary fibre (g)	40	7	5
cholesterol (mg)	0	0	0

This dish is an excellent source of protein, fibre and iron, and a good source of B vitamins. Combined with *chapatis* or brown rice, a *raita* and an Indian salad, it makes an extremely nutritious, low-fat, low-kilocalorie, balanced vegetarian meal.

1 C dried chick-peas (*channa dhal*), soaked overnight (in cold water to cover by 10 cm or 4"), and drained
1 tsp tea-leaves
½ tsp salt
5 C (1.25 L) plus 3 T water
2 T soya oil
¾ tsp cumin seeds

100 g (4 oz or about 1) onion, minced
2.5 cm (1") piece ginger, minced
½ tsp turmeric
½ tsp ground cumin
½ tsp ground coriander
½ tsp *garam masala*
½ tsp ground chilli (cayenne)
1 T fresh coriander, minced

1. Place soaked chick-peas, tea-leaves, salt and 4 C (1 L) water in a saucepan; bring to a boil. Reduce heat to low, partially cover and simmer 1½ hours.

2. In another pot, heat oil over moderate heat; add cumin seeds and stir, then add onion and ginger and fry 7 minutes until golden brown. Mix the turmeric, ground cumin, ground coriander, garam masala and chilli with 3 T water; add to the onion mixture and fry for 1 minute.

3. Add the chick-peas and their cooking liquid, and the remaining cup of water. Bring to a boil, reduce heat to low, cover and cook 30-40 minutes, until chick-peas are tender. Garnish with minced fresh coriander.

INDIAN

Masoor Dhal Curry

(serves 4-6)

	total	1 of 4 portions	1 of 6 portions
kcal	1219	305	203
fat (g)	25	6	4
sodium (mg)	1084	271	181
dietary fibre (g)	57	14	10
cholesterol (mg)	0	0	0

This dish is an excellent source of protein, dietary fibre, B vitamins and iron, and it makes a perfect accompaniment to curry dishes.

230 g (8 oz) orange lentils (*masoor dhal*)
4-5 C (1 L-1.25 L) water
½ tsp salt
2 tsp ground turmeric
½ tsp sugar

40 g (1½ oz or about 4) green chillies, sliced
1½ T soya oil
4 dried red chillies, cut in half
1 tsp fenugreek seeds
300 g (10 oz or 2 medium) onions, minced

1.   Wash lentils and remove any small stones; bring to a boil in 4 C water with the salt and turmeric, then reduce the heat to moderate and cook until the dhal *is somewhat broken up and the texture is soupy. Add more water if necessary. Add sugar and green chillies, stir and remove from heat.*

2.   *In another pot, heat oil and fry dried chillies, fenugreek seeds and onions until the onions are soft and golden. Add this to the* dhal, *and cook over moderate heat until the* dhal *is thickened and soupy.*

INTERNATIONAL

Black Bean Tostadas

(serves 8)

	total	1 of 8 portions
kcal	4162	520
fat (g)	89	11
sodium (mg)	3175	397
dietary fibre (g)	216	27
cholesterol (mg)	121	15

This tasty, substantial Mexican lunch or supper dish is rich in protein, calcium, fibre and iron, and a good source of vitamin C and beta-carotene. To boost nutrition, serve with a fresh carrot and tomato salad sprinkled with lime juice.

1½ T corn or soya oil
1¼ C onion, minced
1 T garlic, minced
800 g (1¾ lb) cooked black beans (if using canned beans, wash and drain well), pounded
½ tsp salt
¼ C (65 ml) water
8 prepared *tostada* shells (available where imported foods are sold)

160 g (5 oz) extra sharp cheddar cheese, grated
8 dark green lettuce leaves, washed and shredded
8 radishes, finely sliced
160 g (5 oz) green capsicum, diced
½ C yoghurt
Mexican sauce (see next recipe)

1. *Heat oil in a heavy skillet with a lid, and fry onion for 7-8 minutes, until soft and golden. Stir in garlic, and cook another 2 minutes. Add the black beans and mash them with the back of a spoon until they are well blended with the onions. Add salt and water, if mixture seems dry; cover the skillet, reduce the heat to very low, and simmer for 5-8 minutes, until heated through.*

2. *Preheat the oven grill or set oven to 230°C (475°F or Gas Regulo 10). To assemble and grill: divide the bean mixture among the 8 tostadas. Sprinkle with equal portions of grated cheese, and place in the oven until cheese is melted. Garnish with shredded lettuce, radishes, capsicum, 1 dollop of yoghurt and another of sauce. Serve with a fresh vegetable salad.*

Mexican Sauce

	total
kcal	153
fat (g)	2
sodium (mg)	37
dietary fibre (g)	27
cholesterol (mg)	0

40 g (1½ oz or about 4) green chillies (*jalapeno* peppers are preferable), seeded and minced
300 g (10 oz) ripe tomatoes, diced
100 g (4 oz) onion, chopped
½ tsp dried oregano
2 tsp fresh lime juice
3 T coriander, chopped

1. *Combine everything in a food processor or blender and chop finely, but do not puree. Transfer to a bowl and chill.*

MALAY

Reduced-Fat Pumpkin and Long Bean Curry

(serves 4-6)

	total	1 of 4 portions	1 of 6 portions
kcal	834	209	139
fat (g)	57	14	10
sodium (mg)	276	69	46
dietary fibre (g)	27	7	5
cholesterol (mg)	55	14	9

This modified version of a Malay favourite — with less than half the fat and kilocalories — is rich in vitamin C and beta-carotene and a fair source of dietary fibre.

1½ T soya oil
10 shallots, pounded
3 red chillies, seeded and pounded
1 tsp shrimp paste (*belacan*), pounded
1 T dried prawns, soaked and pounded
½ C (125 ml) thin coconut milk

3 T evaporated milk mixed with 1½ C (375 ml) water
400 g (14 oz) pumpkin, peeled and cut into 5 cm (2") chunks
150 g (5 oz) long beans, cut into 5 cm (2") pieces

1. *Heat oil over moderate heat and fry pounded ingredients for 4-5 minutes, stirring constantly. Add coconut milk, evaporated milk and water and bring to a boil; add pumpkin and beans and simmer partially covered until vegetables are tender.*

INDIAN

Curried Cauliflower

(serves 4-6)

	total	1 of 4 portions	1 of 6 portions
kcal	717	179	120
fat (g)	34	9	6
sodium (mg)	1185	296	198
dietary fibre (g)	37	9	6
cholesterol (mg)	0	0	0

This dish is delicious, low in kilocalories and high in fibre.

1 T mustard oil
1 T soya oil
¾ tsp mustard seeds
½ tsp cumin seeds
2.5 cm (1") piece ginger, minced
150 g (5 oz or about 1 medium) onion, minced
½ tsp salt
½ tsp turmeric

900 g (about 1¾ lb) cauliflower, trimmed and broken into small flowerets
250 g (8 oz) ripe tomatoes, finely diced
20 g (¾ oz or about 2) green chillies, seeded and minced
¾ tsp ground cumin
½ tsp sugar
2 T fresh coriander, finely chopped
½ C (125 ml) water

1. Heat oils over moderate heat, stir in mustard seeds, then cumin seeds, ginger and onion. Cook 1 minute, stirring constantly, then add salt and turmeric, and cook 3 minutes.

2. Add cauliflower, coating well with onion mixture; then add tomatoes, chillies, ground cumin, sugar and 1 T fresh coriander. Add water, stir, reduce heat to low, and cover. Cook until cauliflower is nearly tender and then remove lid. Continue to cook, stirring frequently, until liquid has mostly evaporated, and cauliflower is tender. Serve garnished with 1 T remaining coriander.

Curried Vegetable Puree
(serves 4-6)

	total	1 of 4 portions	1 of 6 portions
kcal	893	223	149
fat (g)	23	6	4
sodium (mg)	607	152	101
dietary fibre (g)	27	7	5
cholesterol (mg)	0	0	0

This very smooth, tasty, richly coloured vegetable dish is an excellent source of beta-carotene, fibre and vitamin C. It's a perfect dish for children who don't like the texture of whole vegetables. (Note: this dish can be made with fresh mustard greens instead of spinach. Another way to prepare it is to mince the vegetables before cooking, and when tender and nearly dry, to pass the whole mixture through a food mill.)

1 C (250 ml) water
250 g (8 oz) fresh spinach, washed, trimmed and coarsely chopped
250 g (8 oz) fresh broccoli, (including peeled, tender portions of stalks), washed, trimmed and coarsely chopped
1½ T soya oil
2.5 cm (1") piece ginger, minced
100 g (4 oz or about 1) onion, minced
¼ tsp salt
¼ tsp ground cumin
¼ tsp ground turmeric
½ tsp ground coriander
½ tsp *garam masala*

1. Put ½ C (125 ml) water and half the spinach in an electric blender or food processor and blend until spinach is a smooth puree. Add the rest of the spinach, and process the same way. Scrape into a bowl. Put the remaining ½ C (125 ml) water and half the broccoli in the blender and puree; add the remainder. When smooth, add to the pureed spinach.

2. Heat the oil in a karhai, kuali or wok over moderate heat and add the ginger, onion, and salt; fry, stirring constantly, until the onions are golden brown. Add the cumin, turmeric, coriander and garam masala; stir well. Then add the puree and fry 5 minutes.

3. Reduce the heat to low and simmer, uncovered, for 10-15 minutes until almost all liquid has evaporated and the consistency is nearly solid.

INDIAN

Labra (Curried Mixed Vegetables)

(serves 4-6)

	total	1 of 4 portions	1 of 6 portions
kcal	904	226	151
fat (g)	33	8	6
sodium (mg)	1169	292	195
dietary fibre (g)	37	9	6
cholesterol (mg)	0	0	0

This dish is very rich in fibre, vitamin C, beta-carotene and carbohydrate, and low in kilocalories and fat.

2 T soya oil
3-4 dried red chillies
2 tsp *panch masala*
250 g (8 oz) sweet potatoes, peeled and cut into 2.5 cm (1") cubes
150 g (5 oz or about 2 medium) potatoes, peeled and cut into 2.5 cm (1") cubes
110 g (4 oz) pumpkin, peeled and cut into 2.5 cm (1") cubes
110 g (4 oz) cabbage, cut into 2.5 cm (1") pieces

110 g (4 oz or about 2) aubergines (eggplants/brinjals), peeled and cut into 2.5 cm (1") cubes
110 g (4 oz) French beans, stringed and cut in half
4 radishes, cut in half
4 T water
2 tsp ground turmeric
¾ tsp ground chilli (cayenne)
½ tsp sugar
½ tsp salt
20 g (¾ oz or about 2) red chillies, seeded and sliced
1 T coriander leaves, chopped

1. *Heat oil over moderate heat and add dried chillies and* panch masala; *stir until chillies darken. Add all the vegetables and stir for 5 minutes. Add water, turmeric, ground chilli, sugar and salt. Stir again, reduce heat to low, cover pan, and simmer until vegetables are tender, adding gradually a bit of water if vegetables tend to stick. Add sliced red chillies and coriander just before serving.*

INDIAN

Vegetable Khitchri

(serves 8-10)

	total	1 of 8 portions	1 of 10 portions
kcal	2787	348	279
fat (g)	38	5	4
sodium (mg)	1280	160	128
dietary fibre (g)	95	12	10
cholesterol (mg)	0	0	0

This dish is an excellent source of fibre and carbohydrate, and a good source of protein, vitamin C and beta-carotene. It is also very hearty — a little goes a long way to provide good nutrition.

150 g (5 oz) potatoes, scrubbed but not peeled, and diced into 1.25 cm (½") cubes
225 g (8 oz) cauliflower, broken into small flowerets
2 T soya oil
½ tsp cumin seeds
1 stick cinnamon
seeds of 3 cardamom pods
1.25 cm (½") piece fresh ginger, minced
1 bay leaf
2 dried red chillies, seeded and cut into 2.5 cm (1") lengths
200 g (7 oz or about 2) onions, sliced
225 g (8 oz) Basmati rice, washed and drained

350 g (12 oz) green split peas (*moong dhal*), washed
2 tsp ground chilli (cayenne)
2 tsp ground cumin
½ tsp ground turmeric
1 tsp sugar
½ tsp salt
6 C (1.5 L) water
10 whole shallots, peeled
20 g (¾ oz or about 2) red chillies, seeded and sliced
½ C green peas
1 tsp *garam masala*

1. Blanch potatoes and cauliflower in boiling water until partially cooked, and drain. Heat oil in a large, covered saucepan over moderate heat, and fry cumin seeds, cinnamon, cardamom, ginger, bay leaf, dried chillies and onion until onion is softened, about 3 minutes.

2. Add rice, dhal, ground chilli, ground cumin, turmeric, sugar and salt. Stir well and add water; bring to a boil, cover, and cook over low heat. When rice is half done, add potatoes, cauliflower, shallots and sliced red chillies. Cover and continue to simmer until all water is absorbed and rice is fully cooked.

3. Just before serving, stir in the green peas and garam masala.

INDONESIAN

Sayur Assam (Vegetables in Tamarind)

(serves 4-6)

	total	1 of 4 portions	1 of 6 portions
kcal	900	225	150
fat (g)	9	2	2
sodium (mg)	2058	515	343
dietary fibre (g)	41	10	7
cholesterol (mg)	900	225	150

This dish is rich in vitamin C, beta-carotene, dietary fibre, protein and trace minerals, and low in kilocalories and fat.

225 g (8 oz) string beans, stringed and quartered
100 g (4 oz or about 1) onion, minced
4 cloves garlic, minced
4 T tamarind (*assam*) mixed with 5 T water and strained
1 tsp shrimp paste (*belacan*)
1.25 cm (½") piece galingale (*lengkuas*), pounded
2 green chillies, seeded and pounded

4 bird chillies (*chilli padi*), seeded and pounded
4 shallots, peeled and pounded
½ tsp salt
2 C (500 ml) water
450 g (15 oz) prawns, shelled and cleaned
500 g (1 lb) water convolvulus (*kangkong*), trimmed and coarsely chopped
optional: chopped roasted peanuts for garnish

1. *Bring all ingredients except prawns and water convolvulus to a boil; reduce heat, and simmer until beans are tender. Add prawns and water convolvulus and simmer until just done, about 5 minutes. Garnish with chopped roasted peanuts, if desired.*

CHINESE

Vegetarian Wontons

(serves 8)

	total	1 of 8 portions
kcal	1922	240
fat (g)	95	12
sodium (mg)	2527	316
dietary fibre (g)	27	3
cholesterol (mg)	0	0

The filling in this dish freezes very well, and because it makes equally good wontons and *bao*, it's nice to have a supply on hand for last-minute meals. A generous serving has no cholesterol, is low in kilocalories and fat, high in fibre, and a good source of a wide variety of vitamins and minerals.

3 T peanut oil
4 cloves garlic
1.25 cm (½") piece ginger
55 g (2 oz) onion, finely diced
25 g (1 oz) dried Chinese mushrooms, soaked and stemmed
125 g (4 oz) button mushrooms, diced
225 g (8 oz) yambean, finely diced
115 g (4 oz) mock duck (prepared gluten), thoroughly rinsed and finely diced

25 g (1 oz) sweet soyabean wafers (*tim chok*), finely cut
55 g (2 oz) carrots, diced
1 tsp Chinese rice wine
2 tsp light soyasauce
3 tsp dark soyasauce
1 tsp sesame oil
½ C (125 ml) reserved mushroom soaking liquid
1 T cornflour, mixed with 5 T cold water
about 40 prepared wonton skins

1. *Heat oil over moderate heat and fry garlic and ginger until soft; add onions and fry until soft and transparent. Add Chinese and button mushrooms and stir until any moisture has evaporated. Add the yambean, mock duck, sweet soyabean strips, and carrots and stir.*

2. *Add the rice wine, light and dark soyasauces, and sesame oil and stir. Then add the mushroom soaking liquid, and simmer for 10 minutes, until liquid is reduced. Add the cornflour mixture, and simmer until the mixture is well thickened and able to hold its shape well in a spoon. Remove to a bowl and cool.*

3. *When mixture is thoroughly cooled, fill the wontons, placing about 1 tsp of mixture in each. Cover filled wontons with a towel until ready to cook. Drop wontons into boiling stock or water, reduce heat to moderate, and cook until tender, but not falling apart.*

NOTE: This recipe can be used to prepare vegetarian bao. *Use 2 T of filling for each* bao, *place each on a square of greaseproof paper, and steam for 10 minutes.*

INDIAN

Reduced-Fat Vegetarian Cutlets

(serves 6)

	total	1 of 6 portions
kcal	1837	306
fat (g)	63	11
sodium (mg)	1340	223
dietary fibre (g)	54	9
cholesterol (mg)	450	75

This dish is a nutritional power-house: it's low in kilocalories, has less than ⅓ the fat of the original recipe, and it's rich in protein, iron, vitamin C, dietary fibre and beta-carotene.

2 C grated carrots
100 g (4 oz or about 1) onion, minced
2 eggs, lightly beaten
½ C sunflower seeds
¾ C cooked chick peas (*channa dhal*)
½ C cooked orange lentils (*masoor dhal*)
2 tsp parsley, minced
2 tsp coriander, minced

½ tsp ground cumin
½ tsp ground coriander
pinch of *garam masala*
¼ tsp ground chilli (cayenne)
¼ tsp ground black pepper
½ tsp salt
½ tsp soya oil

1. *Mix carrots, onion and eggs. Pound sunflower seeds (or grind them in a blender or food processor) and add to carrot mixture. Pound (or grind) chick peas and orange lentils until coarsely mashed, and add to the carrot mixture along with the parsley, minced coriander, cumin, ground coriander,* garam masala, *chilli, black pepper and salt. Blend thoroughly and chill. Form into cutlets.*

2. *Wipe a non-stick frying pan with a few drops of oil and set over moderate heat. Brown the cutlets a few at a time, turning gently and often, until golden on both sides. Serve hot (or cold in sandwiches); or accompanied by* chapatis, *a vegetable curry or fresh vegetable salad and a portion of* raita *(see recipes pages 114, 77, 148 and 146).*

INTERNATIONAL

Fruit Satay

(serves 4-6)

	total	1 of 4 portions	1 of 6 portions
kcal	447	112	75
fat (g)	2	.5	.3
sodium (mg)	24	6	4
dietary fibre (g)	15	4	3
cholesterol (mg)	0	0	0

Combined with strawberry sauce, these fruit satay sticks make a low-kilocalorie, low-fat dessert that is high in vitamin C, beta-carotene and dietary fibre.

150 g (5 oz) fresh, ripe pineapple, cut into 5 cm (2") cubes
2 kiwi fruits, peeled and cut into 6 wedges each
200 g (7 oz) ripe papaya, cut into 5 cm (2") cubes

1 medium, ripe mango (about 170 g or 6 oz after peeling and discarding the pit), cut into 5 cm (2") cubes
150 g (5 oz) ripe banana, cut into 5 cm (2") pieces
satay sticks

1. Thread the pieces of fruit on satay sticks, alternating each kind. Serve on a platter of cracked or crushed ice, with strawberry sauce (see next recipe).

Strawberry Sauce

	total	1 serving
kcal	192	10
fat (g)	2	.1
sodium (mg)	6	.3
dietary fibre (g)	15	.8
cholesterol (mg)	0	0

2 C fresh, ripe strawberries (substitute: unsweetened, frozen strawberries)
1½ T honey
1 T water
if serving cold: ½ tsp mint leaves, chopped

1. Put strawberries, honey and water in a food processor or blender; blend until smooth.

2. If serving with wholewheat pancakes (see recipe page 113), heat over low heat until warm. If serving as a dessert sauce, add mint leaves and chill thoroughly.

INTERNATIONAL

Low-Fat, High-Fibre Fruit Shakes

(each recipe serves 2-4)

Banana Smoothie

	total	1 of 2 portions	1 of 4 portions
kcal	288	144	72
fat (g)	1	.5	.3
sodium (mg)	104	52	26
dietary fibre (g)	10	5	3
cholesterol (mg)	4	2	1

This absolutely delicious, no-guilt shake is high in vitamin C, dietary fibre, calcium and protein, low in kilocalories and very low in fat.

1 frozen, ripe banana (to freeze: peel, wrap in plastic wrap or tinfoil, and freeze until solid)
¾ C (190 ml) cold skim-milk

½ C fresh, ripe , chilled strawberries (substitute: frozen, unsweetened strawberries, or peeled, diced apples)
1 tsp honey
whole strawberries for garnish

1. *In a blender or food processor, combine banana, milk, strawberries (or apples) and honey; blend until smooth. Serve in chilled glasses, garnished with a whole strawberry slit halfway up to the cap and slipped over the rim.*

Papaya Frappe

	total	1 of 2 portions	1 of 4 portions
kcal	258	129	65
fat (g)	.5	.3	.1
sodium (mg)	17	9	4
dietary fibre (g)	9	5	2
cholesterol (mg)	0	0	0

This is another low-kilocalorie, low-fat winner that is high in beta-carotene, fibre and vitamin C.

2 C ripe, chilled, sweet papaya, peeled,
   seeded and cubed
60 g (2 oz or 1 slice) chilled pineapple, cubed
2 tsp fresh local lime juice (*limau kesturi*)

½ C (125 ml) chilled, unsweetened apple
   juice
pineapple wedges for garnish

1. Combine papaya, pineapple, lime juice and apple juice in a blender or food
    processor. Blend until smooth, and serve in chilled glasses garnished with
    pineapple wedges.

Mango-Yoghurt Shake

	total	1 of 2 portions	1 of 4 portions
kcal	416	208	104
fat (g)	3	2	.8
sodium (mg)	170	85	43
dietary fibre (g)	9	5	2
cholesterol (mg)	11	6	3

This shake is high in vitamin C, beta-carotene and fibre, and a good source of protein, calcium and vitamin B complex.

1 medium, ripe, chilled mango, peeled, pitted
   and cubed
1 small frozen banana

½ C skim-milk yoghurt
½ C (125 ml) skim-milk
papaya wedges for garnish

1. Combine mango, banana, yoghurt and milk in a food processor or blender.
    Blend until smooth, and serve in chilled glasses garnished with papaya
    wedges.

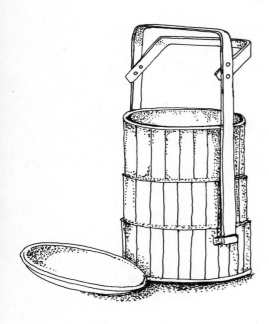

Rice, Noodles, Pastas, Breads and Cereals

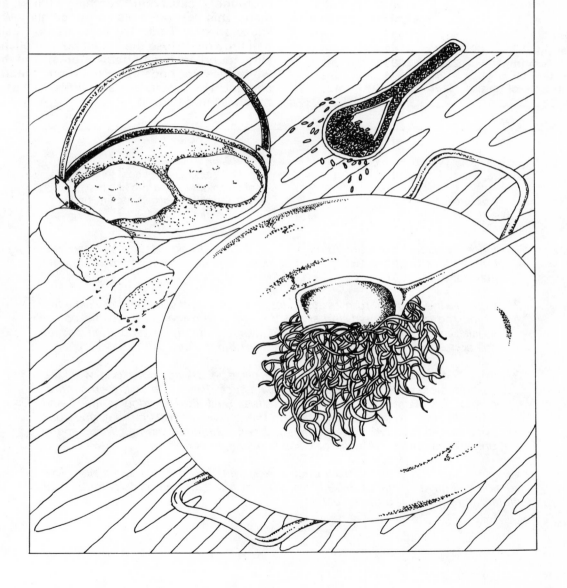

CHINESE

Kai Cheok (Chicken Porridge)

(serves 6-8)

	total	1 of 6 portions	1 of 8 portions
kcal	2827	471	353
fat (g)	78	13	10
sodium (mg)	2335	389	292
dietary fibre (g)	24	4	3
cholesterol (mg)	956	159	120

Porridge is one of the "comfort foods" — profoundly satisfying, soothing, filling and tasty. This version is also surprisingly low in kilocalories and fat. Try the variation using half brown rice (use the hulled but unpolished kind found in health food stores) and half white rice to boost the fibre and vitamin content. The brown rice also adds a pleasant nuttiness and texture.

1 whole chicken, (about 1.5 kg or 3 lb), cleaned, washed, skinned and all visible fat removed
300 g (10 oz) broken rice
1½ T fish sauce

1½ T sesame oil
5 cm (2") piece ginger, finely shredded
4 spring onions, sliced into fine rings
2 fresh red chillies, sliced into fine rings

1. *Place chicken in a snugly fitting pot with 4 C (1 L) cold water, and bring to a boil. Reduce heat to a strong simmer, cover, and cook for 25 minutes, or until just done.*

2. *Remove the chicken from its stock, let stock cool, and skim off any visible fat. Shred the chicken meat and set aside, and return the bones to the pot of stock. Simmer the bones for another 20 minutes, tightly covered, then discard the bones, and again skim off any fat from the surface of the stock.*

3. *Wash rice until water runs clear, and place in a large pot along with the chicken stock, 12 C (3 L) water and fish sauce. Bring to a boil, then simmer briskly, uncovered, about 25-30 minutes, until the porridge is thick and smooth. Add the sesame oil, stir, add the shredded chicken meat, and cook until heated through. Serve garnished with shredded ginger, sliced spring onions and chillies. (A dash of black rice vinegar is optional.)*

Variation: use 150 g (5 oz) brown rice mixed with 150 g (5 oz) white rice. This version will have a total of 2809 kcals, 79 g of fat, 2335 mg of sodium, 29 g of dietary fibre and 956 g of cholesterol.

INDIAN

Saffron Brown Rice Pillau

(serves 6-8)

	total	1 of 6 portions	1 of 8 portions
kcal	2663	444	333
fat (g)	25	4	3
sodium (mg)	143	24	18
dietary fibre (g)	24	4	3
cholesterol (mg)	0	0	0

With less than half the fat, and far fewer kilocalories than the regular recipe, this version is worth a try. The brown rice adds a pleasant, nutty flavour, plenty of fibre and B vitamins.

2 C brown rice
1 T polyunsaturated margarine
½ T soya oil
100 g (4 oz or about 1) onion, minced
50 g (2 oz) sweet red capsicum, finely diced

20 g (¾ oz or about 2) green chillies, seeded and cut into rings
1 stick cinnamon
½ tsp saffron
4 C (1 L) salt-free chicken stock (see recipe page 140)

1. *Wash and drain the rice. Melt the margarine with the oil in a saucepan over moderate heat; fry the onion, sweet capsicum, green chillies, and cinnamon until onion is soft and golden brown.*

2. *If using a rice cooker: place rice, fried mixture, saffron and stock in cooker, cover and steam until done. Stir the rice thoroughly before serving.*

3. *If using a saucepan: add the rice to the fried onion mixture, and fry gently until rice is coated with oil. Add saffron and stir, then add stock and bring to a boil. Cover tightly and steam over lowest heat for 40-45 minutes, or until all liquid is absorbed. Stir before serving.*

MALAY

Easy Lontong (Compressed Rice)

(serves 4-6)

	total	1 of 4 portions	1 of 6 portions
kcal	2031	508	339
fat (g)	4	1	.7
sodium (mg)	513	128	86
dietary fibre (g)	13	3	2
cholesterol (mg)	0	0	0

This rice dish, eaten in every Malay home during Hari Raya, is rich in carbohydrates.

3 C broken rice
water to cover rice by 5 cm (2")

¼ tsp salt
2 screwpine (*pandan*) leaves, tied in a knot

1. *Cook rice in water with salt and screwpine leaves for about 20 minutes over moderate heat, until water is absorbed, but rice is still moist. Pound the rice a little with a wooden spoon to make it even finer. Let rice cool thoroughly until no steam is left.*

2. *Use 2 flat pans: in the larger, press the rice down firmly, and cover with plastic wrap. The smaller pan should be .6 cm (about ¼") or so smaller all around, and should fit snugly inside the larger. Place this on top of the rice, and set heavy weights on top to compress the rice. Refrigerate for 8 hours or overnight; slice into squares. Serve with Reduced-Fat Tempe Goreng (see recipe page 62), or any dish desired.*

MALAY

Reduced-Fat Nasi Goreng (Fried Rice)

(serves 6)

	total	1 of 6 portions
kcal	3073	512
fat (g)	92	15
sodium (mg)	478	80
dietary fibre (g)	36	6
cholesterol (mg)	479	80

This version of a classic dish cuts the fat in half and adds more low-fat protein. It makes an excellent meal when combined with a dark green or deep yellow vegetable like water convolvulus (*kangkong*) or pumpkin. It's rich in carbohydrate, a good source of protein, and a fair source of vitamin B complex and trace minerals.

6 C cold, cooked rice
1 egg, lightly beaten
3 T soya oil
10 shallots, coarsely chopped
3 cloves garlic, minced
3 red chillies, seeded and sliced

60 g (2 oz) prawns, shelled and coarsely chopped
150 g (5 oz) chicken breast, cut into 1.25 cm (½") pieces
60 g (2 oz) green peas
3 spring onions, sliced into fine rings

1. *Fluff up the rice with a fork to separate grains. Set a non-stick frying pan over moderately high heat, and when hot, add the beaten egg, swirling the pan around to coat thinly. Continue to cook, swirling the pan until the omelette is thin and barely dry on top. Immediately peel off the omelette, and let it cool for 1 minute. Roll into a tight cylinder, and cut crosswise into thin slices. Put shreds aside for garnish.*

2. *Wipe out the pan, set it over moderately high heat, and add the oil. When hot, fry the shallots, garlic and chillies until the shallots are soft; add the chopped prawns and chicken, and fry until the chicken turns white and firm and the prawns turn pink. Add the rice and peas, and stir-fry with a wooden spoon until the rice is heated through and well blended with seasonings. Garnish with shredded omelette and sliced spring onions.*

Nasi Kunyit (Turmeric Rice)

(serves 4-6)

	total	1 of 4 portions	1 of 6 portions
kcal	1547	387	258
fat (g)	12	3	2
sodium (mg)	1010	253	168
dietary fibre (g)	18	5	3
cholesterol (mg)	5	1	.8

This version has much less saturated fat, total fat and kilocalories than the original recipe.

2 C glutinous rice, thoroughly washed
4 cm (1½") piece fresh turmeric, pounded
  and tied in a piece of muslin (substitute: 1
  tsp ground)

screwpine (*pandan*) leaves
½ tsp salt
3 T evaporated milk
2 T thick coconut milk

1. *Place rice, turmeric bag or dried turmeric and boiling water to cover in a deep bowl. Let stand 10 hours or overnight, covered. Drain liquid and rinse rice. Place screwpine leaves at the bottom of a metal or bamboo steamer, and place soaked rice on top. Steam over boiling water for 5 minutes. Make holes in the rice with a chopstick (to help steam circulate), and steam a further 45 minutes.*

2. *Remove rice to a bowl, add salt, evaporated milk, and coconut milk and mix well. Return to the steamer for 5 more minutes.*

Maze Gohan (Mixed Rice and Vegetables)

(serves 4-6)

	total	1 of 4 portions	1 of 6 portions
kcal	2513	628	419
fat (g)	18	5	3
sodium (mg)	1514	379	252
dietary fibre (g)	20	5	3
cholesterol (mg)	0	0	0

This colourful, delicate, yet filling family-style dish makes a simple meal when accompanied by a light soup and a Japanese salad. It provides fair amounts of protein, B vitamins, calcium, phosphorus, beta-carotene and vitamin C, and is an excellent source of carbohydrate.

3 C (750 ml) *niban dashi* (see recipe page 135)
2 T *mirin* (sweet *sake*)
½ tsp salt
1 tsp light soyasauce
3 C Japanese rice (substitute: Australian short-grain), soaked 3 hours in water to cover
1 large *shiitake* mushroom, soaked in hot water and trimmed

115 g (about 4 oz) *konnyaku* (gelatinous root vegetable), thinly sliced, shredded, blanched and drained
50 g (2 oz) carrot, shredded
12 ginko nuts, cooked, peeled, and bitter centres removed by driving a wooden toothpick through the oval ends of each nut
100 g (4 oz) *kamaboko* (Japanese fishcake), thinly sliced
½ C green peas

1. *In a large pan combine the* niban dashi, mirin, *salt, soyasauce and rice; stir well and bring to a boil. Add the* shiitake *mushroom,* konnyaku, *carrot, ginko nuts, and* kamaboko; *stir, reduce the heat to low, cover the pan and simmer until all the liquid is absorbed. Stir in the green peas, cover again and simmer an additional 2 minutes.*

INTERNATIONAL

Brown Rice with Mint and Peas
(serves 6)

	total	1 of 6 portions
kcal	1571	262
fat (g)	18	3
sodium (mg)	476	79
dietary fibre (g)	31	5
cholesterol (mg)	0	0

This dish is rich in carbohydrate, thiamine, niacin and dietary fibre.

2 C long-grain brown rice, washed
water to cover by 5 cm (2") or to the 2 C (500 ml) mark in an electric rice cooker
1 T polyunsaturated, soft, tub-type margarine

1 T fresh mint leaves, minced (substitute: 1 tsp dried mint leaves)
150 g (5 oz) green peas

1. *If using a saucepan: bring rice and water to a boil; reduce heat to very low, cover tightly, and cook 40-45 minutes, until rice is tender and liquid is absorbed. (It is easier to use a rice cooker.)*

2. *5 minutes before cooking time is up, stir in the margarine, mint leaves and peas; cover and cook until done.*

INTERNATIONAL

Brown Rice Pudding

(serves 6-8)

	total	1 of 6 portions	1 of 8 portions
kcal	2211	369	276
fat (g)	15	3	2
sodium (mg)	767	128	96
dietary fibre (g)	24	4	3
cholesterol (mg)	247	41	31

Feed this dish to children to introduce them to the nutritional benefits of brown rice. It's rich in protein, iron and vitamin B complex, and a good source of carbohydrate and dietary fibre.

½ C skim-milk powder
¼ C palm sugar (*gula melaka*), grated
1 tsp ground cinnamon
½ tsp ground nutmeg
2 ½ C (725 ml) skim-milk
1 whole egg plus 1 egg white

1 tsp vanilla
2 C cooked brown rice
2 T raisins
¼ C dried papaya, coarsely chopped
¼ C dried apricots, coarsely chopped
1 6 C (1.5 L) baking dish or casserole, oiled

1. *Preheat oven to 165°C (325°F or Gas Regulo 5). Combine the skim-milk powder, palm sugar, cinnamon and only ¼ tsp nutmeg. Add the skim-milk, egg, egg white and vanilla, and mix well. Add the rice, raisins, papaya and apricots. Blend well and pour into the baking dish or casserole. Sprinkle with remaining ¼ tsp nutmeg.*

2. *Bake for 15 minutes, stir, then bake an additional 25-35 minutes, or until all the milk is absorbed. Do not bake the rice pudding until completely dry as it will continue to absorb liquid as it cools. Serve warm or cold.*

INTERNATIONAL

Tomato Rice

(serves 6-8)

	total	1 of 6 portions	1 of 8 portions
kcal	1693	282	212
fat (g)	46	8	6
sodium (mg)	1549	258	194
dietary fibre (g)	8	1	1
cholesterol (mg)	0	0	0

This dish is rich in carbohydrate, protein, vitamin A, vitamins B2, B6 and B12, and niacin, as well as being low in kilocalories and fat.

300 g (10 oz) rice, washed and drained
2⅓ C (600 ml) water
1 T tomato puree
1 T tomato ketchup

¼ tsp salt
200 g (7 oz) water-packed tuna-fish, drained
　and rinsed of brine
coriander, coarsely chopped

1. *Cook rice in water until almost done; stir in the tomato puree, ketchup and salt. Continue cooking until rice is tender. Serve topped with flaked tuna-fish and coriander.*

CHINESE

Vegetarian Reduced-Fat Fried Bee Hoon

(serves 4-6)

	total	1 of 4 portions	1 of 6 portions
kcal	1170	293	195
fat (g)	49	12	8
sodium (mg)	3968	992	661
dietary fibre (g)	54	14	9
cholesterol (mg)	0	0	0

This dish is an excellent source of carbohydrates and fibre, and a good source of beta-carotene and vitamin C. It contains half the fat of the regular recipe, no cholesterol, and still has plenty of good flavour.

3 T soyabean oil
5 red chillies (about 50 g or 2 oz), pounded
3 cloves garlic, pounded
4 slices green ginger, pounded
1½ T preserved soyabeans (*taucheo*), rinsed thoroughly
1 carrot (about 70 g or 2½ oz), peeled and shredded
150 g (5 oz) cabbage, shredded

10 French beans, (about 80 g or 3 oz), trimmed and sliced diagonally into 2.5 cm (1") pieces
15 snowpeas (about 50 g or 2 oz), stringed
¾ tsp salt
1¾ C (400 ml) water
250 g (8 oz) rice vermicelli (*bee hoon*), soaked in boiling water 3 minutes and drained
150 g (5 oz) bean sprouts, washed and tailed
2 tsp light soyasauce

1. *Heat oil over moderate heat, and fry the pounded chilli, garlic, ginger and preserved soyabeans for 2 minutes. Add the carrot, cabbage, beans and snowpeas and stir-fry for another 2 minutes.*

2. *Add salt and water and simmer gently for 4 minutes. Add noodles and bean sprouts and toss together over moderate heat until heated through and well combined with other ingredients. Add a little extra water if mixture is too dry; taste for seasoning, and if necessary, add up to 2 tsp light soyasauce.*

Cantonese Noodle Soup

(serves 4-6)

	total	1 of 4 portions	1 of 6 portions
kcal	968	242	161
fat (g)	32	8	5
sodium (mg)	1456	364	243
dietary fibre (g)	10	3	2
cholesterol (mg)	278	70	46

This dish is low in kilocalories and fat, and a good source of trace elements, protein and fibre.

2 T soya oil
1 clove garlic
4 ½ C (1.1 L) water
100 g (4 oz) kale (*kailan*), cut diagonally into 5 cm (2") lengths
100 g (4 oz) cuttlefish, sliced
100 g (4 oz) prawns, shelled

50 g (2 oz) sliced garoupa (or threadfin/*ikan kurau*)
200 g (7 oz) rice flour noodles (*hor fun*)
2 tsp fish sauce
1 tsp ground black pepper

1. *Heat oil and fry garlic until brown. Add water and bring to a boil. Add kale, cuttlefish, prawns, and fish and simmer until fish and prawns begin to turn opaque.*

2. *Add noodles, fish sauce and black pepper, and simmer 2 minutes. (Optional: garnish with sliced fresh red, or pickled green chillies.)*

MALAY

Laksa Assam

(serves 6)

	total	1 of 6 portions
kcal	1290	215
fat (g)	9	2
sodium (mg)	712	119
dietary fibre (g)	106	18
cholesterol (mg)	48	8

My version of this well-loved classic is low in kilocalories and fat, a good source of carbohydrate and vitamin C, and a fair source of protein, B vitamins and beta-carotene.

600 g (1 ¼ lb) mackerel (*ikan tenggiri* or *ikan parang*)
7 C (1.75 L) water
13 red chillies, seeded and pounded
2 stems lemon grass (*serai*), sliced and pounded
2.5 cm × 2.5 cm × .5 cm (1″ × 1″ × ¼″) piece shrimp paste (*belacan*), pounded
6 pieces dried tamarind slices (*assam gelugor* or substitute: 5 T tamarind mixed with ½ C/125 ml water)
handful of *laksa* leaves (*daun kessom*), washed and stripped from stems

250 g (8 oz) thick rice (*laksa*) noodles, soaked 30 minutes (if purchased dried)
125 g (4 oz or half a medium) cucumber, peeled and shredded
150 g (5 oz) pineapple, shredded
1 ginger flower (*bunga kantan*), shredded (if unavailable, leave out)
2 red chillies, sliced
1 C mint leaves, washed and dried
1 red onion, cut into thin wedges
2 limes, quartered
1 T black prawn paste mixed with 2 T water

1. *Bring the fish to a boil in the water, simmer until just cooked. Remove, flake flesh from the bones and set aside. Add the pounded ingredients to the fish stock along with the tamarind and* laksa *leaves; simmer gently. Meantime, boil the rice noodles in another pot until soft. (If you purchase fresh noodles, simply drop them into boiling water for 2 minutes, and drain.)*

2. *Arrange the cucumber, pineapple, ginger flower, chillies, mint, onion and limes on a serving platter. Return the flaked fish to the gravy, and simmer 3 minutes. Place equal portions of noodles in each of 6 soup bowls, fill with gravy, and pass the platter of vegetables and prawn paste as garnishes.*

MALAY

Mee Siam (Spicy Noodles)

(serves 4-6)

	total	1 of 4 portions	1 of 6 portions
kcal	2658	665	443
fat (g)	75	19	13
sodium (mg)	1750	438	292
dietary fibre (g)	37	9	6
cholesterol (mg)	736	184	123

Low in kilocalories and fat, this version of Mee Siam is a fair source of protein, vitamins C and A, dietary fibre and iron.

10 dried chillies, soaked and seeded
12 shallots
1 stem lemon grass (*serai*), sliced
½ tsp shrimp paste (*belacan*)
2 tsp salted soyabeans (*taucheo*), rinsed and drained
3 tsp sugar
3 T soya oil
½ C tamarind (*assam*) mixed with 4 C (1 L) water and strained
2 T coconut milk mixed with 2 T evaporated milk

2 pieces firm soyabean curd (*taukwa*), sliced into .6 cm (¼") pieces
200 g (7 oz) bean sprouts
200 g (7 oz) water convolvulus (*kangkong*), coarsely chopped
250 g (8 oz) cooked prawns, coarsely chopped
1 C chives, chopped
500 g (1 lb) rice vermicelli (*bee hoon*), soaked in boiling water for 10 minutes and cut into 6 cm (2 ½") pieces
1 hard-boiled egg, sliced
6-8 local limes (*limau kesturi*), halved and seeded

1. *Pound together: dried chillies, shallots, lemon grass, shrimp paste, salted soyabeans, sugar, and 1½ T soya oil.*

2. *Heat 1 T soya oil in a kuali or wok over moderate heat; add pounded ingredients and fry 3 minutes, stirring constantly. Reserve half for the sauce, and set the kuali with the remainder aside.*

3. *To make the sauce: add the tamarind water, coconut milk and evaporated milk to the reserved fried ingredients. Bring nearly to a boil, then simmer for 5 minutes and set aside.*

4. *In a non-stick pan, heat the remaining ½ T oil and fry the firm soyabean curd slices until golden. Set aside.*

5. *Return the kuali and its ingredients to moderate heat, then add the bean sprouts, water convolvulus, half the prawns and half the chives. Cook for 1-2 minutes, then begin adding the rice vermicelli, stirring to blend well. When all the noodles are completely heated, serve topped with the soyabean curd slices, remaining prawns and chives and sliced egg; sprinkle with lime juice. Pass the sauce separately.*

JAPANESE

Hiyashi Somen (Ice-Cold Summer Noodles)

(serves 6-8)

	total	1 of 6 portions	1 of 8 portions
kcal	648	108	81
fat (g)	.3	.05	.04
sodium (mg)	14	2	2
dietary fibre (g)	13	2	2
cholesterol (mg)	0	0	0

These noodles are very refreshing in hot weather. For a cooling, nutritious meal, combine them with a Japanese salad, a light soyabean curd dish (made with silken *tofu*) garnished with grated ginger, toasted *katsuobushi* (bonito fish flakes), sliced spring onions, and a dash each of soyasauce and *su* (rice vinegar). The *menrui no dashi* adds some protein, niacin, vitamins B1, B12 and B6, pantothenic acid, folacin and choline.

8 C (2 L) water
450 g (15 oz) *somen* (thin white Japanese noodles)

16-18 ice cubes
2.5 cm (1") grated ginger
2 T spring onions, finely sliced

1. Bring the water to a boil; add noodles, return to the boil, and cook for 6 minutes, stirring occasionally. Drain, immerse in cold water and drain again. Divide the noodles among 6-8 serving bowls and drop 2 or 3 ice cubes in each.

2. Serve with individual bowls of menrui no dashi *(see next recipe)* and condiment dishes each containing a portion of the grated ginger and sliced spring onions.

Menrui No Dashi

	total
kcal	203
fat (g)	.2
sodium (mg)	2148
dietary fibre (g)	0
cholesterol (mg)	0

¼ C (65 ml) *mirin* (sweet *sake*)
2 ½ T light soyasauce
1 C (250 ml) *niban dashi* (see recipe page 135)
2 T flaked *katsuobushi* (dried bonito)

1. Heat the mirin *in a small saucepan, then turn off the heat and carefully ignite with a match. Shake the pan gently until the flame dies out. Add soyasauce,* dashi, katsuobushi *and bring to a boil. Strain immediately, and cool to room temperature.*

JAPANESE

Zarusoba (Buckwheat Noodles)

(serves 6-8)

	total	1 of 6 portions	1 of 8 portions
kcal	1667	278	208
fat (g)	7	1	.9
sodium (mg)	11	2	1
dietary fibre (g)	23	4	3
cholesterol (mg)	0	0	0

This is one of the best noodle dishes there is: it is a good source of carbohydrate and a fair source of fibre, trace minerals, calcium and iron.

8 C (2 L) water
450 g (15 oz) *soba* (buckwheat noodles)
3 sheets *nori* (dried laver seaweed), passed over a flame on one side, and coarsely crumbled

4 spring onions, cut into thin rings
4 tsp *wasabi* (horseradish powder), mixed with just enough water to make a thick paste, and formed into 6-8 small balls

1. Bring water to a boil in a heavy pot. Add soba, *and stirring occasionally, cook for 7 minutes until tender. Drain immediately, and immerse in cold water. Drain thoroughly, and divide among 6-8 bowls or curved Japanese bamboo noodle baskets.*

2. *Garnish each portion with crumbled* nori *and spring onions, and provide each diner with a deep bowl of dipping sauce and a condiment dish containing a ball of* waṣabi.

Dipping Sauce (Soba Tsuyu)

	total
kcal	207
fat (g)	.2
sodium (mg)	2576
dietary fibre (g)	0
cholesterol (mg)	0

¼ C (65 ml) *mirin* (sweet *sake*)
3 T light soyasauce
1 C (250 ml) *niban dashi* (see recipe page 135)
2 T flaked *katsuobushi* (dried bonito)

1. Heat mirin *in a small saucepan, turn off the heat, then carefully ignite with a match, and shake the pan until the flame dies out. Add the soya,* dashi, *and* katsuobushi *and bring to a boil. Immediately strain the sauce and cool to room temperature.*

JAPANESE

Su Udon (Noodles in Broth)

(serves 6-8)

	total	1 of 6 portions	1 of 8 portions
kcal	725	121	91
fat (g)	1	.2	.1
sodium (mg)	2031	339	254
dietary fibre (g)	12	2	2
cholesterol (mg)	0	0	0

This beautifully delicate dish (perfect for lunch or supper) is a good source of carbohydrate, protein and trace minerals.

8 C (2 L) water
400 g (14 oz) *udon* (wide noodles)
6 C (1.5 L) *ichiban dashi* (see recipe page 134)
3 tsp sugar

½ tsp salt
3 tsp soyasauce
4 spring onions, sliced into thin rounds

1. *Bring water to boil in a large pot with a lid. Add the noodles, return to the boil, and stirring occasionally, cook briskly for about 15-20 minutes, until noodles are very soft. Turn off the heat, cover the pan, and let rest 5 minutes. Drain, and cool noodles under cold running water. Drain again and set aside.*

2. *Combine dashi, sugar, salt, soyasauce and bring to a boil in a large pot. Add the drained noodles, and return to the boil. Divide the noodles and soup among individual bowls. Garnish with spring onions.*

Variation: Tsukimi Udon — garnish each bowl with a raw egg and a little crumbled nori *(dried laver seaweed); the heat from the soup will lightly cook the egg. This version has a total of 809 kilocalories, 7 grams of fat, 2117 milligrams of sodium, 12 grams of fibre and 225 milligrams of cholesterol.*

INTERNATIONAL

Wholegrain Pasta with Tomato-Mint Sauce
(serves 6-8)

	total	1 of 6 portions	1 of 8 portions
kcal	1048	175	131
fat (g)	38	6	5
sodium (mg)	1244	207	156
dietary fibre (g)	22	4	3
cholesterol (mg)	0	0	0

This dish — quick and surprisingly easy to prepare — is rich in carbohydrate, fibre, vitamin C, vitamin B1, niacin and beta-carotene. When accompanied by a salad topped with a few slices of hard-boiled egg or a few sardines, it makes a delicious, well-balanced, low-kilocalorie, low-fat meal.

4 C imported, tinned, Italian plum tomatoes, pureed with their liquid in a food mill or food processor
2 T polyunsaturated, soft, tub-type margarine
1¼ T fresh mint, chopped (substitute: 1½ tsp dried)
½ tsp salt

1 tsp sugar
freshly ground black pepper
20 C (5 L) water
1 bay leaf
500 g (1 lb) wholegrain spaghetti
whole mint leaves and a sprinkling of grated *parmesan* cheese for garnish

1. *Put the pureed tomatoes, margarine, mint, salt and sugar in a saucepan. Bring to a boil over moderate heat, then reduce the heat to low, and simmer uncovered for 10 minutes, stirring occasionally. Add black pepper to taste.*

2. *Meanwhile, bring water and bay leaf to a rolling boil in a large pot with a lid. Add pasta, stir well to make sure it doesn't stick, cover and return to the boil. When water boils a second time, uncover the pot and boil over high heat for 8-10 minutes, until the pasta is* al dente *— cooked, but still slightly resistant to the bite.*

3. *When pasta is cooked, drain thoroughly in a colander, place on a serving platter, and pour sauce over. Garnish with whole mint leaves and a sprinkling of grated* parmesan *cheese.*

INTERNATIONAL

Vegetarian Spinach Lasagne

(serves 8-10)

	total	1 of 8 portions	1 of 10 portions
kcal	2970	371	297
fat (g)	110	14	11
sodium (mg)	4428	554	443
dietary fibre (g)	34	4	3
cholesterol (mg)	106	13	11

This delicious dish is an Italian family-style favourite, but nice enough to serve for company. It's quite low in kilocalories and fat, and a good source of vitamin C, beta-carotene, fibre, calcium, protein and vitamins B1, B2 and B12.

Vegetables:

100 g (4 oz or 2 small) zucchini, sliced into .6 cm (¼") rounds

70 g (2 ½ oz or 2 ribs) celery, stringed, and sliced into .6 cm (¼") pieces

100 g (4 oz) small brinjal (eggplant/aubergine), sliced into .6 cm (¼") rounds

1 tsp salt

150 g (5 oz) broccoli, stems removed, broken into small flowerets

150 g (5 oz) fresh button mushrooms, sliced into .6 cm (¼") pieces

White Sauce (Besciamella):

4 T polyunsaturated, soft, tub-type margarine

5 T plain, all-purpose flour

1 C skim-milk powder, mixed with 3 C (750 ml) water

¼ tsp freshly grated nutmeg (substitute: ground)

ground white or black pepper to taste

Other ingredients:

3 C pizza sauce (see recipe page 111)

300 g (10 oz or about 21 pieces) pre-cooked, dried, spinach lasagne noodles

½ C grated *parmesan* cheese

1 32 cm × 23 cm × 12 cm (13" × 9" × 5") pan

1. *To make the vegetables: put zucchini, celery and brinjal into a colander or strainer; add salt and toss vegetables until well coated. Let rest for 30 minutes, until the moisture has left the vegetables. Then flush with cold water to remove all the salt, and press the vegetables dry between paper towels. Set aside.*

2. *Drop the broccoli into boiling water and blanch for 3 minutes. Drain, cool, and dry completely. Set aside with other vegetables.*

3. *Grill the mushroom slices over moderate heat in a dry non-stick pan until dry and slightly brown. Add to other vegetables.*

4. To make the white sauce: heat the margarine over moderate heat until melted and all foam has subsided; add the flour and stir constantly for 3 minutes. Add the skim-milk powder mixed with water all at once, beating with a wire whisk to prevent any lumping.

5. Bring the sauce to a boil over moderate heat, whisking constantly. When it has thickened to a smooth heavy cream consistency, add the nutmeg and pepper, reduce the heat to low and simmer 3 minutes, stirring constantly. Remove from heat. (If sauce thickens too much while resting, thin with a little skim-milk.)

6. Preheat the oven to 190°C (375°F or Gas Regulo 7). To assemble the lasagne: spread a thin layer of pizza sauce on the bottom of the pan; place 7 noodles on top of the sauce, edges slightly overlapping. Top the noodles with a layer of white sauce, and over that scatter ½ the vegetables. Add a little pizza sauce to moisten the vegetables.

7. Place another layer of 7 noodles topped with pizza sauce in the pan. Then scatter in the remaining vegetables, cover with another layer of noodles, and top with a layer of pizza sauce and a layer of white sauce. (Take care not to mix the tomato sauce with the white sauce.) Sprinkle the top with ½ C grated parmesan *cheese.*

8. Bake for 30-40 minutes, taking care not to let the top or edges burn. When the pan is bubbling and the white sauce is lightly browned, the lasagne is ready. Serve with a fresh green salad.

INTERNATIONAL

Baked Wholegrain Macaroni and Cheese

(serves 6-8)

	total	1 of 6 portions	1 of 8 portions
kcal	1437	240	180
fat (g)	62	10	8
sodium (mg)	2075	346	259
dietary fibre (g)	5	.8	.6
cholesterol (mg)	92	15	12

A little of this dish goes a long way — it can be used as a main course for lunch or supper or as a side dish. It's high in carbohydrate, fibre, vitamin B1, niacin, calcium and protein.

2 C (500 ml) white sauce (see recipe page 106 and steps 4 and 5 on page 107)
1½ C extra-sharp cheddar cheese, grated
250 g (8 oz) wholegrain macaroni (or any short, tubular wholegrain pasta), cooked in boiling water for about 8 minutes until barely tender, drained and cooled

freshly ground black pepper
cayenne pepper or paprika
1 souffle dish or casserole, lightly oiled

1. Preheat oven to 175°C (350°F or Gas Regulo 6). Heat white sauce and add 3 T grated cheddar cheese; stir until melted. Mix in macaroni and toss well.

2. Put a layer of macaroni in the casserole, dust with black pepper and cayenne or paprika, then add a layer of grated cheese. Continue layering until all ingredients are used up (about 3 layers), ending with cheese. Bake for about 30 minutes until bubbling hot and lightly browned.

INTERNATIONAL

Stuffed Pasta Shells

(serves 8-10)

	total	1 of 8 portions	1 of 10 portions
kcal	2058	257	206
fat (g)	90	11	9
sodium (mg)	4441	555	444
dietary fibre (g)	153	19	15
cholesterol (mg)	406	51	41

This dish is rich in carbohydrate, a good source of protein, calcium, iron, vitamin C and beta-carotene, and reasonably low in kilocalories and fat. It tastes even better the second day.

Filling:

115 g (4 oz) low-fat *mozzarella* cheese, cut into 6 cm (¼") cubes
450 g (about 1 lb) cottage cheese
¼ C grated *parmesan* cheese
1 egg, lightly beaten
3 shallots, minced
2 tsp fresh basil or parsley, minced
¼ tsp freshly grated nutmeg (substitute: ground nutmeg)
¼ tsp salt
freshly ground black pepper

about 20 pieces jumbo pasta shells, cooked in boiling water until barely tender and quite resistant to the bite, and drained
2 C pizza sauce (see recipe page 111)
1 32 cm × 23 cm × 12 cm (13" × 9" × 5") baking pan

1. Preheat oven to 175°C (350°F or Gas Regulo 6). Combine the mozzarella, cottage cheese, parmesan, egg, shallots, basil or parsley, nutmeg, salt and pepper to taste, and blend well. Stuff shells with mixture. (Shells should fit the baking pan in a single layer.)

2. Place 1 C pizza sauce over the bottom of the baking pan; put the stuffed shells on top, and drip the remaining sauce over. Bake for about 30 minutes, or until the cheese has melted, and the sauce is bubbling hot.

INTERNATIONAL

Wholegrain Pizza with Low-Fat Toppings

(makes four 25 cm or 10" pizzas, four slices in each)

	total	1 pizza	1 slice
kcal	4263	1066	266
fat (g)	176	44	11
sodium (mg)	4991	1248	312
dietary fibre (g)	243	61	15
cholesterol (mg)	288	72	18

This excellent, relatively low-fat, low-kilocalorie Italian meal is high in carbohydrate, fibre and protein, a fair source of calcium, and an excellent source of vitamins C and A. (The chart includes nutritional information for pizza, sauce and all the toppings except the optional tuna and sardines.)

Crust:

1¼ C (315 ml) skim-milk
2 T active dry yeast
1 tsp honey (substitute: sugar)
3 T sesame paste (*tahini*), available at health food stores
1 T soya oil
2 C wholewheat flour
1½ C plain, all-purpose flour
1 large baking sheet or pizza pan, sprinkled with cornmeal or plain, unsweetened wheat germ

3 C pizza sauce (see next page)

Toppings:

2 C shredded, low-fat *mozzarella* cheese
350 g (12 oz) fresh, ripe tomatoes, thinly sliced
350 g (12 oz) mushroom slices, grilled (in a non-stick pan)
350 g (12 oz) green capsicum, thinly sliced
350 g (12 oz) red capsicum, thinly sliced
4 T grated *parmesan* cheese
(optional: 200 g or 7 oz water-packed flaked tuna and 2 T rinsed brisling sardines)

1. Heat milk until just lukewarm, and pour into a large bowl. Sprinkle on the yeast, add the honey, stir, and set in a draft-free, warm place for 5-7 minutes, until the yeast has bubbled up and doubled in volume. (If yeast doesn't activate, start again.) Add the sesame paste and oil.

2. To the yeast mixture, add the wholewheat flour, a little at a time, and enough plain flour to form a non-sticky dough. Turn the dough out on a lightly floured surface, and knead by hand for about 15 minutes, until smooth, elastic and shiny, adding more plain flour as needed.

3. Put the dough in a large, oiled bowl, turning it to oil all surfaces. Cover and allow to rise about 90 minutes in a warm, draft-free place until doubled in bulk while you make the pizza sauce (see next recipe).

4. Punch down, and divide dough into 4 pieces. Knead each piece for a minute, then flatten each into 15 cm (6") rounds. Cover with a tea towel, and let rest 15 minutes while you preheat the oven to 230°C (450°F or Gas Regulo 10).

5. Roll each round into a 25 cm (10") circle. Place each circle on a baking sheet or pizza pan sprinkled with cornmeal or wheat germ, and make the edges of the dough thick enough to contain the sauce and toppings. Spread each crust with ¾ C pizza sauce, and top with ½ C shredded mozzarella. Add toppings.

6. Let rest for 5 minutes, then bake, one pizza at a time, on the lowest shelf or the floor of the oven for 8-10 minutes, rotating the pizza once during the baking to ensure an even, golden crust.

7. Keep warm while you bake the rest of the pizzas, or divide into 4 sections, and serve at once.

INTERNATIONAL

Pizza Sauce

(yields 3 cups)

	total
kcal	648
fat (g)	31
sodium (mg)	68
dietary fibre (g)	149
cholesterol (mg)	0

This Italian sauce can be used for pizza, Vegetarian Spinach Lasagne (see page 106), or Stuffed Pasta Shells (see page 109). The sauce freezes well, so it is a good idea to make extra.

2 T olive oil (extra virgin olive oil is preferable)
150 g (5 oz or about 2 medium) onions, minced
1 T garlic, minced
4 C imported, tinned, Italian plum or whole tomatoes, coarsely chopped, but not drained
1 170 g (6 oz) tin tomato paste

1 T dried oregano, crumbled
1 T fresh basil, minced (substitute: 1 tsp dried basil, crumbled)
1 bay leaf
2 tsp sugar
½ tsp salt
freshly ground black pepper

1. Heat the olive oil over moderate heat in a large saucepan, and fry the minced onions, stirring frequently for 7 minutes, until soft. Add the garlic and stir for 1 minute.

2. Add the tomatoes and their liquid, the tomato paste, oregano, basil, bay leaf, sugar, salt, and black pepper to taste. Bring to a boil, reduce the heat to very low, and simmer, uncovered, stirring occasionally, for about 1 hour. The finished sauce should be quite thick and smooth. To use in pizza, Vegetarian Spinach Lasagne or Stuffed Pasta Shells, allow to cool before using.

111

INDIAN

Thosai

(makes 10-12 pieces)

	total	1 of 10 pieces	1 of 12 pieces
kcal	2726	273	227
fat (g)	35	4	3
sodium (mg)	1149	115	96
dietary fibre (g)	79	8	7
cholesterol (mg)	225	23	19

This dish is one of my favourites — it makes a wonderful breakfast dish when served with *sambar* (see recipe page 130). In Singapore, *thosai* is traditionally served with coconut sambal, which is high in saturated fat and kilocalories. *Sambar* adds fibre, vitamins and minerals and, combined with the complete vegetable protein in the *thosai*, provides an excellent, low-fat vegetarian meal.

1 C black gram dhal (*urad dhal*), washed and
   small stones discarded
2 C uncooked rice
water
½ tsp salt
a good pinch of yeast
rice flour
1½ T soya oil
1 egg

Optional ingredients:

½ C onions, finely minced
¼ C coriander, finely minced
2 T ginger, minced
20 g (¾ oz or about 2) green chillies, minced

1. *Start the night before: soak the* dhal *in water to cover 8 hours or overnight. Soak the rice in a separate bowl overnight.*

2. *In the morning: rub off the black* dhal *skins between your hands, and discard them. Grind the* dhal *to a paste with about ½ C (125 ml) water in a blender, food processor or* batu giling.

3. *Grind the rice to a paste with about ½ C (125 ml) water. Put ground rice, ground* dhal, *salt, and enough water to make the batter the consistency of heavy cream in a large pot or bowl and blend well. Add a pinch of yeast, stir again, and cover. Let rest at room temperature 12 hours, or overnight, until the batter has risen and gives off a yeasty, fermented aroma.*

4. *When ready to cook, add small amounts of water or rice flour to adjust the consistency of the batter to that of heavy cream. At this point, you may add all or some of the optional ingredients listed above, if desired.*

5. *Heat a cast iron skillet or tawa over moderate heat, until quite hot. Add soya oil, and when hot, fry the egg, folding and turning it, so it absorbs all the oil. Place the fried egg in a paper towel or piece of muslin, and use it to lightly oil the tawa as you cook each* thosai.

6. *Fill a ladle with about ¼-½ C batter, and quickly pour it into the centre of the tawa. Swirl the batter out from the centre with the back of the ladle, until you have a circle about 18 cm (7") in diameter. (Experienced cooks can cover the whole tawa.) Cook over moderate heat until the surface bubbles and the edges are dry; turn quickly and carefully with a metal spatula or pancake turner, and cook another 30-45 seconds.*

7. *Remove each thosai to a plate while you cook the rest, lightly greasing the tawa each time. Serve with sambar or spiced potatoes with mustard seed as a filling (see recipes pages 130 and 71).*

INTERNATIONAL

Wholewheat Pancakes

(yields 20)

	total	1 pancake
kcal	1710	86
fat (g)	56	3
sodium (mg)	1301	65
dietary fibre (g)	11	.6
cholesterol (mg)	462	23

These pancakes make a wonderful Sunday breakfast treat — if you skip the syrup and honey and stick with low-kilocalorie strawberry sauce (see recipe page 85). They're rich in carbohydrate, fibre and thiamine, and a good source of protein, calcium, iron, vitamins B2 and B12, biotin, folic acid and choline.

2 C wholewheat flour
¼ C plain, all-purpose flour
½ C unsweetened wheat germ
2 tsp baking powder

2 eggs, lightly beaten (or 1 whole egg plus 1 egg white)
2 ½ C (625 ml) skim-milk
2 T soya oil

1. *Combine flours, wheat germ, baking powder, and blend well. In another bowl, combine the eggs, milk and oil; add the wet ingredients to the dry, and stir just long enough to combine. Do not over-mix — the batter should be slightly lumpy.*

2. *Heat a lightly oiled griddle or tawa over moderate heat; pour about ¼ C (65 ml) batter for each pancake. When the surface bubbles burst, and the bottom of the pancake is browned, turn and cook until the other side is browned. Serve hot, with warm strawberry sauce.*

INDIAN

Whole-meal Chapatis
(makes 12 chapatis)

	total	1 chapati
kcal	833	69
fat (g)	22	2
sodium (mg)	985	82
dietary fibre (g)	6	.5
cholesterol (mg)	0	0

Chapatis are an excellent source of carbohydrate, and a good source of B vitamins and fibre. Fortunately, they are also low in kilocalories and fat. This recipe looks like more work than it really is. You can mix and knead the dough in the morning before work, and roll and cook the *chapatis* before dinner. Or, mix and knead after dinner in the evening, and roll and cook the *chapatis* during the daytime. I usually double the recipe because *chapatis* tend to disappear quickly. They make a very important nutritional contribution, particularly to vegetarian meals.

2 C whole-meal wheat flour (*atta*)
½ tsp salt
2 tsp soya oil

about ½ C (125 ml) lukewarm water
¼ C extra flour for dusting while rolling

1. *Start the morning or night before: put flour and salt in a bowl and mix well. Rub in the soya oil and then begin adding the water, while mixing and kneading with your hands. You should have a soft, slightly sticky dough that will become smooth and shiny as you work it. You may need slightly less or slightly more water, depending on the flour and the weather. If the dough sticks to your hands after one minute of kneading, add a little more flour.*

2. *Knead the dough for at least 10 minutes, until it is smooth, shiny and elastic. Shape dough into a ball, place in a bowl, and cover with plastic wrap. Let dough rest in refrigerator all day or overnight, (or 3 hours at room temperature, covered with a damp tea towel). Chapatis are lighter in texture when dough rests overnight.*

3. *Use about 2 T dough for each* chapati*; shape into round balls, then roll out on a floured surface into circles about 15-18 cm (6"-7") in diameter. Keep the rolled* chapatis *covered with a tea towel while you roll the rest.*

4. *Heat a cast-iron frying pan or tawa over moderate heat until very hot. Put a* chapati *on the tawa, and move it around with your fingers until brown spots appear. Turn the* chapati *over and, with a folded tea towel, gently press around the edges. The centre will puff up. Remove and allow to cool while you cook the rest.*

Bran Muffins

(yields 24 muffins)

	total	1 muffin
kcal	1604	67
fat (g)	57	2
sodium (mg)	3146	131
dietary fibre (g)	21	.9
cholesterol (mg)	231	10

Terrific for breakfast along with a glass of orange juice and some plain, skim-milk yoghurt, these muffins are high in carbohydrate, fibre, vitamin B complex, protein and calcium, and relatively low in kilocalories and fat. They also make a healthy after-school snack for children along with a glass of plain skim-milk. Don't use butter or margarine — the muffins are rich enough without it.

1½ C plain bran flakes
1¼ C (315 ml) skim-milk
¾ C plain, all-purpose flour
¾ C wholewheat flour
2 ½ tsp baking powder
½ tsp salt

3 T soya oil
¼ C unsulphured molasses (available in
  health food stores)
1 T honey
1 egg, lightly beaten
24 muffin cups, oiled, or muffin pans, oiled

1.   *Preheat oven to 205°C (400°F or Gas Regulo 8). Combine bran flakes and milk; let stand 10 minutes. In another bowl, combine flours, baking powder and salt. In a third bowl, combine the oil, molasses, honey and egg, and blend in the bran and milk mixture. Mix well.*

2.   *Add the flour mixture to the bran mixture, stirring just long enough to thoroughly moisten. Do not over-mix, or muffins will be full of tunnels and holes. Fill muffin tins or prepared muffin cups ⅔ full and bake for 20-30 minutes.*

Variation: add ½ C raisins to batter before baking.

INTERNATIONAL

Sweet Cornbread

(yields about 10 slices)

	total	1 slice
kcal	1678	168
fat (g)	70	7
sodium (mg)	2334	233
dietary fibre (g)	11	1
cholesterol (mg)	230	23

This cornbread can be eaten as a lightly sweet cake or as an accompaniment to bean and rice dishes. It toasts well (but use a little honey or jam instead of butter), it's high in carbohydrate, and a fair source of fibre, beta-carotene, protein and B complex vitamins.

1 C (250 ml) skim-milk
1 egg, lightly beaten
¼ C (65 ml) soya oil
1 C yellow cornmeal
½ C plain, all-purpose flour
½ C wholewheat flour

¼ C sugar
4 tsp baking powder
¼ tsp salt
1 greased 20 cm (8") square baking pan

1. *Preheat oven to 220°C (425°F or Gas Regulo 9). Combine wet ingredients: mix milk, egg and soya oil.*

2. *Combine dry ingredients: mix cornmeal, flours, sugar, baking powder and salt. Add the wet ingredients to the dry, and beat for 1 minute, until batter is fairly smooth. Bake for 10 minutes, then reduce heat to 205°C (400°F or Gas Regulo 8) and bake for 10 minutes more, tenting loosely with tinfoil if cornbread appears to be browning. Do not allow cornbread to brown. Cool completely on a wire rack before slicing.*

Savoury Corn Pudding with Chillies and Cheese
(serves 6-8)

	total	1 of 6 portions	1 of 8 portions
kcal	4865	811	608
fat (g)	125	21	16
sodium (mg)	6977	1163	872
dietary fibre (g)	62	10	8
cholesterol (mg)	711	119	89

This dish — high in fibre, carbohydrate, protein, iron, calcium, pantothenic acid, and vitamins B1, B2 and B12, and a fair source of iron — makes a light luncheon dish, or a substantial grain side dish at dinner. It's very filling, so keep portions small.

1 C yellow cornmeal
½ tsp baking powder
¾ tsp baking soda
½ tsp salt
500 g (1 lb) corn kernels, (frozen is preferable to tinned)
4 spring onions, finely sliced
4 green chillies, seeded and minced

260 g (8 oz) Danish Havarti (or Monterey Jack) cheese; 1 C diced, the remainder grated
2 eggs, lightly beaten
1½ C (375 ml) skim-milk mixed with ¾ C skim-milk yoghurt
1 20 cm × 20 cm × 5 cm (8" × 8" × 2") baking dish, lightly oiled

1. Preheat oven to 220°C (425°F or Gas Regulo 9). Put the empty baking dish into the oven to heat. Then combine dry ingredients: mix cornmeal, baking powder, baking soda and salt.

2. Combine wet ingredients: mix corn, spring onions, chillies, diced cheese, eggs, skim-milk and yoghurt. Pour wet ingredients into dry, and stir just until combined. Do not beat.

3. Scrape pudding mixture into the hot baking dish, top with grated cheese, and bake for about 25 minutes until golden brown, firm, but still slightly soft in the centre. Serve with a fresh vegetable salad.

INDIAN

Farina with Vegetables (Uppuma)

(serves 4-6)

	total	1 of 4 portions	1 of 6 portions
kcal	1224	306	204
fat (g)	34	9	6
sodium (mg)	1063	266	177
dietary fibre (g)	25	6	4
cholesterol (mg)	0	0	0

This dish makes a delectable, hearty breakfast, a carbohydrate and fibre-rich side dish, or a light lunch or supper when combined with yoghurt and *dhal*. With a fair amount of vitamin C and beta-carotene, it's one of my favourite dishes.

2 T soya oil
1 T black gram dhal (*urad dhal*)
1 tsp mustard seeds
150 g (5 oz or about 1 medium) onion, minced
10 g (about 1) green chilli, seeded and minced
1 C quick-cooking farina (*rava*)
150 g (5 oz) tomatoes, finely diced and minced

70 g (2½ oz or about 1 large) carrot, finely diced
4 spring onions, sliced
3 C (750 ml) water
½ tsp salt
1 T coriander leaves, finely chopped
1 T fresh lemon juice

1.	Heat oil over moderate heat and add dhal *and mustard seeds; when seeds pop, add onions and fry 7 minutes, until golden brown. Add the chilli, and then pour the farina in slowly.*

2.	*Add tomatoes, carrot, spring onions, water and salt, stirring constantly. Bring to a boil, then reduce the heat to low, cover and simmer over very low heat, stirring frequently to prevent sticking. Serve when the farina is thick and the vegetables are cooked, about 5-10 minutes. Garnish with coriander and sprinkle with lemon juice.*

INTERNATIONAL

High-Fibre Breakfast

(serves 1-2)

	total	1 of 2 portions
kcal	579	290
fat (g)	20	10
sodium (mg)	229	115
dietary fibre (g)	10	5
cholesterol (mg)	11	6

This breakfast provides you with all you need to start the day: plenty of energy and good nutrition. It's high in carbohydrates, fibre and protein, and a good source of trace minerals and calcium. The fruit adds vitamin C and beta-carotene.

30 g (1 oz) oatmeal
30 g (1 oz) unsweetened wheat germ
40 g (about 1½ oz) mixed raw white sesame seeds, sunflower seeds, pumpkin seeds and raisins

½ C (125 ml) skim-milk
½ C skim-milk yoghurt
100 g (4 oz) either papaya, mango, banana, cantaloupe or apple, or a mixture

1. *Mix dry ingredients in serving bowls; combine skim-milk and yoghurt, and pour over dry ingredients, blending well. Add fruit (and a little more milk, if mixture is dry), and serve. (If you simply must have it sweetened, add a little unsweetened apple juice to the dry ingredients.)*

119

INTERNATIONAL

Oatmeal Porridge

(serves 6-8)

	total	1 of 6 portions	1 of 8 portions
kcal	1993	332	249
fat (g)	26	4	3
sodium (mg)	513	86	64
dietary fibre (g)	38	6	5
cholesterol (mg)	0	0	0

If using rolled oats:

2¼ C rolled oats
5 C (1.25 L) cold water
¼ tsp salt

1. Place rolled oats, water and salt in a heavy saucepan with a lid. Bring to a boil over moderate heat, stirring frequently. Reduce heat to low, and simmer, stirring frequently, until the porridge is creamy. Cover the pan, remove from heat, and let rest for 5 minutes.

2. Serve hot, with skim-milk, sliced fresh fruit (or stewed, dried prunes or apricots), wheat germ and cinnamon topping. (The milk and fruit add protein, vitamin C, beta-carotene and calcium.)

	total	1 of 6 portions	1 of 8 portions
kcal	1328	221	166
fat (g)	17	3	2
sodium (mg)	504	84	63
dietary fibre (g)	25	4	3
cholesterol (mg)	0	0	0

If using quick-cooking oats:

3½ C (875 ml) boiling water
¼ tsp salt
1½ C quick-cooking oats

1. Bring water and salt to a boil in a heavy saucepan with a lid. Add the oats, and cook over moderate heat, stirring frequently, for 3-5 minutes. Remove from heat, cover, and let rest 5 minutes.

2. Serve hot, with skim-milk, sliced fresh fruit (or stewed, dried prunes or apricots), wheat germ and cinnamon topping. (The milk and fruit add protein, vitamin C, beta-carotene and calcium.)

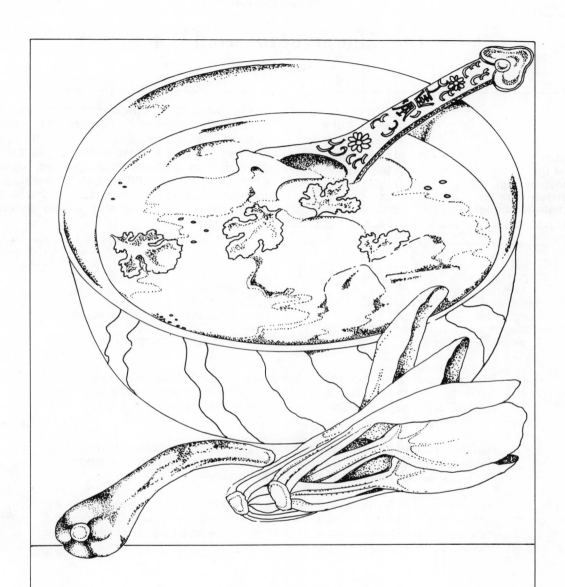

Soups, Stews and Salads

SINGAPOREAN

Chicken and Macaroni Soup

(serves 8)

	total	1 of 8 portions
kcal	1661	208
fat (g)	56	7
sodium (mg)	2015	252
dietary fibre (g)	24	3
cholesterol (mg)	820	103

Using wholegrain macaroni improves the nutritional content of this home-style favourite, and removing the skin from the chicken reduces the fat content. The dish is also rich in carbohydrate, protein, dietary fibre, vitamins B1, B6 and B12, niacin, pantothenic acid, folacin and choline. For a balanced meal, serve with a vegetable dish or a fresh salad.

8 C (2 L) water
1 T whole peppercorns
½ tsp salt
1 tsp sugar
1.3 kg (about 3 lb) chicken, skinned and all
  visible fat removed

1 tsp light soyasauce
½ tsp sesame oil
225 g (8 oz) wholegrain macaroni
40 g (1½ oz or about 4) red chillies, seeded
  and sliced
1 bunch coriander, chopped

1. *In a saucepan large enough to comfortably hold the chicken and water, boil the water with the peppercorns, salt and sugar; add the chicken, and return to the boil. Immediately reduce the heat to very low, cover the pan, and simmer for 35 minutes.*

2. *Remove the chicken, and when cool enough to handle, shred the meat from the bones and mix with the soyasauce and sesame oil. Return the bones to the stock, and simmer uncovered for 1½ hours.*

3. *Remove the pot from the heat and strain the stock, discarding the bones and peppercorns. Add the macaroni and return to high heat until done (about 8 minutes). Serve in individual bowls and garnish with shredded chicken, sliced chillies, and chopped coriander.*

CHINESE

Sweet-Corn and Chicken Soup

(serves 4-6)

	total	1 of 4 portions	1 of 6 portions
kcal	2053	513	342
fat (g)	23	6	4
sodium (mg)	882	221	147
dietary fibre (g)	13	3	2
cholesterol (mg)	146	37	24

This is a rich soup, so a small portion is sufficient. It's a good source of dietary fibre, beta-carotene and carbohydrate, and a fair source of protein, phosphorus, thiamine, riboflavin and iron.

150 g (5 oz) boneless, skinless chicken breast
1 egg white
3 C (750 ml) chicken stock
450 g (about 1 lb) creamed sweet-corn

2 tsp soyasauce
1 tsp sesame oil
freshly ground black pepper to taste
1 T cornflour mixed with 2 T water

1. *Mince chicken, and mix with egg white and only 3 T stock. Set aside.*

2. *Combine the remaining stock, the sweet-corn, soyasauce, sesame oil and pepper in a saucepan and bring to a boil. After the mixture has boiled for three minutes, add the cornflour mixture, stirring constantly.*

3. *When the soup is thickened and boiling, add the chicken mixture, stirring constantly, and remove the pan from the heat as soon as the soup returns to the boil. Serve immediately.*

CHINESE

Fishball and Tang Hoon Soup

(serves 4-6)

	total	1 of 4 portions	1 of 6 portions
kcal	1006	252	168
fat (g)	13	3	2
sodium (mg)	1855	464	309
dietary fibre (g)	30	8	5
cholesterol (mg)	275	69	46

Low in kilocalories and packed with good nutrition, this soup makes an excellent light luncheon or supper dish. It is an excellent source of protein, a good source of niacin and a fair source of vitamin C, beta-carotene and fibre.

500 g (1 lb) fishballs, (see recipe below or use commercially-prepared)
1 T oil
2 cloves garlic, finely sliced
4 C (1 L) light fish stock or water
150 g (5 oz) water convolvulus (*kangkong*), cut into 5 cm (2") pieces

90 g (3 oz) transparant noodles (*tang hoon*), soaked in hot water for 15 minutes, then cut into 10 cm (4") pieces
40 g (1½ oz) red chilli, sliced
a pinch each of chopped Chinese celery, chopped coriander leaves, chopped spring onion and ground black pepper for garnish

1. *Use the fishheads and bones from the fishball recipe below to make a light stock; otherwise, use commercially-prepared fishballs and water.*

2. *Heat oil and fry garlic slices until golden brown. Add stock/water, and bring to a boil. Add the fishballs and simmer for 10 minutes; then add the water convolvulus and noodles and cook just until the vegetable is slightly wilted. Serve garnished with red chilli, celery, coriander, spring onion and black pepper to taste.*

Fishballs

	total
kcal	521
fat (g)	11
sodium (mg)	1766
dietary fibre (g)	0
cholesterol (mg)	275

500 g (1 lb) white fleshed fish fillets like wolf herring (*ikan parang*), Spanish mackerel (*ikan tenggiri*), sea bream or red snapper (*ikan merah*)
½ tsp salt mixed with 6 T water
white pepper
1 tsp cornflour

1. If using a batu lesong: *chop fish meat finely with a cleaver. Pound and add the salted water a little at a time, until the mixture is smooth and firm. Add the white pepper and cornflour, and mix well.*

2. If using a food processor: *process 2.5 cm (1") cubes of fish meat until finely minced; add the pepper, cornflour and only 4 T salted water, and process until smooth.*

3. To form fishballs: *take a fistful of fish mixture, and squeeze a lump through the hole formed by your thumb and forefinger. Scrape off 2 cm (¾") balls with a spoon, and store in lightly salted water until ready to use.*

Variation: add finely chopped chillies to the fishball mixture.

CHINESE

Bird's Nest and Chicken Soup

(serves 4-6)

---

	total	1 of 4 portions	1 of 6 portions
kcal	1145	286	191
fat (g)	36	9	6
sodium (mg)	1698	425	283
dietary fibre (g)	0	0	0
cholesterol (mg)	637	159	106

This soup is light, delicate and perfect for the sick. It is an excellent source of protein, and a good source of phosphorus, calcium, iron, thiamine and riboflavin.

---

50 g (2 oz) bird's nest
1 whole chicken (about 1 kg or 2.2 lb)

4 C (1 L) water
½ tsp salt

1. Clean bird's nest: *soak in water until soft, then pick out any traces of foreign matter with a pair of tweezers. Wash bird's nest in several changes of water until absolutely clean.*

2. *Remove the head and wing tips from the chicken and discard; remove all skin and visible fat and wash chicken well. Cut chicken into bite-sized pieces, discarding the backbone with its reddish glands.*

3. *Place all ingredients in double boiler and steam for two hours. Skim off all visible fat and serve.*

CHINESE

Lohan Chai (Vegetarian Stew)

(serves 10-12)

	total	1 of 10 portions	1 of 12 portions
kcal	2133	213	178
fat (g)	62	6	5
sodium (mg)	8901	890	742
dietary fibre (g)	56	6	5
cholesterol (mg)	0	0	0

This is a beautifully rich dish — fragrant and smoky — with the added benefit of being low in kilocalories and fat, and high in fibre, thiamine, niacin, riboflavin, iron, calcium and phosphorus. Leftovers are no problem with this dish — the flavour seem to deepen and intensify the longer it sits.

40 ginko nuts (50 g or 2 oz)
40 lotus seeds (50 g or 2 oz)
3 T soya oil
60 g (2 oz) ginger, bruised
4 pieces preserved red bean curd (*foo yu*), mashed
12 dried Chinese mushrooms (50 g or 2 oz), soaked and stemmed
300 g (10 oz) Chinese cabbage, cut into 5 cm (2") pieces
4 sweet soyabean wafers (*tim chok*) (25 g or 1 oz), soaked in warm water until soft, drained and cut into 5 cm (2") pieces
100 g (4 oz) golden needles (tigerlily buds), hard tips discarded, soaked in warm water until soft, and drained

100 g (4 oz) tinned button mushrooms, drained
120 g (4 oz) transparent vermicelli (*bee hoon*), soaked in warm water until soft and drained
25 g (1 oz) hair vegetable (*fatt choy*), soaked in warm water, rinsed and drained
20 red dates (50 g or 2 oz), washed and drained
3 T cloud ear fungus, soaked in warm water until soft and drained
3 T hoisin sauce
3 T oyster sauce
1 T sugar
7½ C (2 L) water

1. *Prepare the ginko nuts: tap each nut sharply along its ridged edge to crack the shell. Drop nuts into boiling water and boil for 2-3 minutes; when shelled, the brown skin over each nut should slip off easily. Next, remove the bitter central core of each nut by pushing a wooden toothpick through the pointed end and out the rounded end. The bitter core should pop out.*

2. *Prepare the lotus seeds: soak the seeds in plenty of warm water for 1 hour and then rub off the thin brown skins that cling to each seed. Seeds will separate into two halves after soaking.*

3. *Heat the oil in a large pot over moderate heat; add the ginger and fry until fragrant. Add most of the mashed preserved bean curd, and fry 30 seconds. Add all remaining ingredients except the sauces, sugar and water, and stir well. Then add the hoisin and oyster sauces, the sugar and water, and simmer gently, partially covered, for one hour. The stew should be very thick, with just a moderate amount of liquid. Taste and adjust seasoning if necessary by adding more preserved bean curd, oyster sauce or hoisin sauce.*

CHINESE

Egg Drop Soup

(serves 4-6)

	total	1 of 4 portions	1 of 6 portions
kcal	1069	267	178
fat (g)	6	2	1
sodium (mg)	559	140	93
dietary fibre (g)	.5	.1	.08
cholesterol (mg)	225	56	38

This soup is simplicity itself. Quick and easy to prepare, delicate and delicious, it is a fair source of protein, iron and B vitamins.

3 C (750 ml) salt-free chicken stock (see recipe page 140)
¼ tsp salt (optional)

1 T cornflour dissolved in 2 T cold water
1 egg, lightly beaten
1 spring onion, finely sliced

1. Bring stock and salt (if used) to a boil; add cornflour paste and stir until the stock thickens slightly and becomes clear.

2. Slowly pour in the beaten egg, and stir twice, gently. Remove pot from heat, and serve immediately, garnished with sliced spring onion.

CHINESE

Watercress and Sweet Date Soup

(serves 4-6)

	total	1 of 4 portions	1 of 6 portions
kcal	198	50	33
fat (g)	2	.5	.3
sodium (mg)	147	37	25
dietary fibre (g)	17	4	3
cholesterol (mg)	0	0	0

The tang of the watercress in this soup contrasts nicely with the sweetness of the dates. It is a fair source of vitamin C, beta-carotene, dietary fibre and iron.

300 g (10 oz) watercress, coarsely chopped, tough stems discarded

10 sweet dates, washed
6 C (1.5 L) water

1. Bring all ingredients to a boil, then reduce heat and simmer very gently for one hour. You may need to replenish water if too much boils away.

INDIAN

Lamb Soup with Lentils and Vegetables

(serves 4-6)

	total	1 of 4 portions	1 of 6 portions
kcal	1577	394	263
fat (g)	71	18	12
sodium (mg)	1441	360	240
dietary fibre (g)	23	6	4
cholesterol (mg)	356	89	59

This soup is an excellent source of protein, and a good source of vitamin C, beta-carotene, B vitamins and iron.

8 C (2 L) water
5 cloves garlic, minced
2.5 cm (1″) piece ginger, minced
150 g (5 oz or 1 medium) onion, coarsely chopped
1 stick cinnamon
3 tsp ground coriander
6 cardamom pods, crushed
½ C orange lentils (*masoor dhal*), washed and small stones discarded

2 tsp ground cumin
1 tsp black peppercorns, pounded
½ tsp salt
450 g (about 1 lb) lean lamb (substitute: mutton), cut into 5 cm (2″) cubes
170 g (6 oz or about 2) tomatoes, quartered
3 spring onions, coarsely chopped
1 T coriander leaves, chopped

Fishball and Tang Hoon Soup, page 124

Chicken Masala, page 24, Carrot Pachadi, page 68, and Cabbage and Carrot Salad, page 147

Sambar, page 130, Rasam (Pepper Soup), page 129, and Thosai, page 112

Curried Cauliflower, page 78, Mint and Onion Raita, page 146, Masoor Dhal Curry, page 75, Tomato, Onion and Beet Salad, page 148, and Whole-meal Chapatis, page 114

1. Boil water with garlic, ginger, onion, cinnamon, 2 tsp coriander, cardamom, lentils, cumin, black pepper and salt. Add lamb and cook over moderate heat, partially covered until lamb is tender and liquid reduced to about 3 C (750 ml).

2. Add tomatoes, spring onions, and remaining 1 tsp ground coriander, and simmer until tomatoes are tender, about 7 minutes. Serve garnished with chopped coriander leaves.

INDIAN

Rasam (Pepper Soup)

(serves 4-6)

	total	1 of 4 portions	1 of 6 portions
kcal	724	181	121
fat (g)	20	5	3
sodium (mg)	1020	255	170
dietary fibre (g)	20	5	3
cholesterol (mg)	0	0	0

This low-fat, low-kilocalorie soup goes very well with Southern Indian curries. It is a good source of protein, fibre, B vitamins and iron, and a fair source of vitamin C and beta-carotene.

½ C yellow lentils (*channa dhal*), washed, soaked in water to cover for 1 hour and drained
3 C (750 ml) water
¼ tsp cumin
½ tsp black peppercorns, pounded
¼ tsp ground turmeric
½ tsp salt
4 cloves garlic, crushed

100 g (4 oz) ripe tomato, pounded
¼ tsp asafoetida
3 tsp tamarind (*assam*), soaked in 4 T water and strained
3 tsp soya oil
½ tsp mustard seeds
4 shallots, finely sliced
1 sprig curry leaves (*karuvapillai*)
1 dried red chilli, seeded and broken into 1.25 (½") pieces

1. Bring lentils and water to a boil; reduce heat to low and simmer 30 minutes. Drain off the cooking liquid and save; discard the lentils.

2. Bring lentil water, cumin, black pepper, turmeric, salt, garlic, tomato, asafoetida, and tamarind to a boil, then simmer for 15 minutes, stirring occasionally.

3. Heat oil over moderate heat, and add the mustard seeds, shallots, curry leaves and dried red chilli. When chilli turns brown, add this mixture to the simmering soup. Return to the boil, and serve hot.

INDIAN

Sambar

(serves 6-8)

	total	1 of 6 portions	1 of 8 portions
kcal	2464	411	308
fat (g)	77	13	10
sodium (mg)	1165	194	146
dietary fibre (g)	71	12	9
cholesterol (mg)	0	0	0

This soup is very rich in dietary fibre, a good source of protein, B vitamins and iron, and a fair source of beta-carotene. Try it with *thosai*, (see recipe page 112) or *chapatis* (see recipe page 114). It makes a hearty breakfast, and a light lunch or supper dish.

1½ C orange lentils (*masoor dhal*)
1.25 cm (½") piece ginger, sliced
5 cloves garlic, halved
8 shallots, finely sliced (substitute: red onion)
20 g (¾ oz or about 2) green chillies, quartered
½ tsp salt
1 tsp soya oil
½ tsp ground turmeric
150 g (5 oz or about 2) white potatoes, scrubbed, unpeeled and quartered
60 g (2 oz or 1 large) carrot, sliced 1.25 cm (½") thick
60 g (2 oz) lady's fingers (okra), cut into 4 cm (1½") lengths

20 g (¾ oz or about 4) green beans, cut into 4 cm (1½") pieces
70 g (2 ½ oz or about 1 small) aubergine (brinjal/eggplant), quartered
170 g (6 oz or about 2) ripe tomatoes, quartered
3 T tamarind (*assam*) soaked in ½ C (125 ml) water and strained
1 T soya oil
½ tsp mustard seed
2 dried red chillies, seeded and cut into 2.5 cm (1") lengths
1 sprig curry leaves (*karuvapillai*)

1. Wash lentils and discard any small stones. Place in a saucepan with ginger, garlic, 4 sliced shallots/red onions, green chilli, salt, oil, turmeric and enough water to cover by 5 cm (2"). Bring to a boil, then reduce heat to low and simmer until lentils are quite soft.

2. Add potatoes, carrot, lady's fingers, green beans, aubergine, and tomatoes, and simmer until vegetables are tender. Add tamarind water and more water, if necessary.

3. Heat oil and fry mustard seeds, chillies, curry leaves and remaining four sliced shallots/red onions for 3 minutes. Add to the vegetable mixture, and continue to cook 5 minutes. Serve with thosai *(see recipe page 112)*.

INDONESIAN

Soto Ayam (Chicken and Noodle Soup)

(serves 6-8)

	total	1 of 6 portions	1 of 8 portions
kcal	1466	244	183
fat (g)	63	11	8
sodium (mg)	1632	272	204
dietary fibre (g)	6	1	.8
cholesterol (mg)	627	105	78

This nutritious, home-style meal is quite simple to make, rich in protein, phosphorus and carbohydrate and a fair source of thiamine, riboflavin and iron.

60 g (2 oz) transparent noodles (*tang hoon*), soaked, drained and cut into 5 cm (2") lengths
1 kg (2.2 lb) chicken, skinned, all visible fat removed, and cut into 8 pieces
150 g (5 oz or 1 medium) onion, quartered
4 T Chinese celery with leaves, chopped
½ tsp salt
8 C (2 L) water

1½ T soya oil
2 bay (*salam*) leaves
2 stems lemon grass (*serai*), crushed
4 cloves garlic, minced
1.25 cm (½") piece ginger, minced
½ tsp ground turmeric
1 hard-boiled egg, finely chopped
2 spring onions, sliced into fine rings

1. Let the noodles soak while you prepare the chicken. Place chicken, onion, celery and salt in a heavy saucepan with a lid. Add water, bring to a boil, reduce heat to low, cover partially, and simmer 30 minutes. Remove chicken, strain stock, and strip the chicken meat from the bones. Shred the chicken meat.

2. In the same saucepan (washed and thoroughly dried), heat the oil over moderate heat. Add the bay leaves, lemon grass, garlic, ginger and turmeric, and stir for 3 minutes. Add the strained chicken stock, the noodles and chicken; bring to a boil, then reduce heat and simmer 5 minutes. Garnish with chopped egg and spring onions.

MALAY

Reduced-Fat Sop Kambing (Lamb Soup)

(serves 4-6)

	total	1 of 4 portions	1 of 6 portions
kcal	990	248	165
fat (g)	58	15	10
sodium (mg)	1358	340	226
dietary fibre (g)	6	2	1
cholesterol (mg)	287	72	48

This version has much less saturated fat, total fat and kilocalories than the original recipe. It's also a good source of protein, vitamin B complex, iron and zinc.

2 T soya oil
150 g (5 oz or about 1 medium) onion, finely
   sliced
1.25 cm (½") piece ginger, pounded
6 cloves garlic, pounded
1 stem curry leaves
1 stick cinnamon
2 green cardamom pods, smashed
3 whole cloves
350 g (12 oz) lamb, cut into 2.5 cm (1") cubes,
   (mutton is acceptable, but not preferred)

1½ tsp freshly ground black pepper
½ tsp ground chilli (cayenne)
1 T ground coriander
¾ tsp ground cumin
½ tsp salt
5¼ C (1.3 L) water
½ C (125 ml) thin coconut milk mixed with 2
   T evaporated milk
6-8 local limes (*limau kesturi*), halved

1. Heat oil over moderate heat and fry onions, ginger, garlic, curry leaves, cinnamon, cardamom and cloves, stirring constantly for 3 minutes. Add the lamb cubes, black pepper, ground chilli, coriander, cumin and salt, and fry over low heat until the lamb is coated with spices. Add water, bring to a boil, reduce heat to low, partially cover pan and simmer until lamb is tender.

2. Remove cover, add coconut milk mixed with evaporated milk, stir to blend well, and simmer an additional 20-30 minutes. Skim off all visible fat. Garnish with limes.

JAPANESE

Miso Shiru (Clear Soup with Soyabean Paste)

(each soup serves 6)

Red Miso:

	total	1 of 6 portions
kcal	306	51
fat (g)	5	.8
sodium (mg)	14	2
dietary fibre (g)	33	6
cholesterol (mg)	0	0

White Miso:

	total	1 of 6 portions
kcal	440	73
fat (g)	12	2
sodium (mg)	14	2
dietary fibre (g)	51	9
cholesterol (mg)	0	0

Rich in protein, fibre, B vitamins and trace minerals, these soups are important elements of a Japanese meal. They add to and complement nutritional values and bring balance and flavour. The red variety is usually served in summer and the white variety in winter.

Red Miso:

6 C (1.5 L) *ichiban dashi* (basic stock — see recipe page 134)
½ C red soyabean paste

White Miso:

6 C (1.5 L) *ichiban dashi* (basic stock — see recipe page 134)
1 C white soyabean paste

Possible Garnishes:

wakame (dried seaweed) and thinly sliced spring onions
tofu (diced into .6 cm or ¼" cubes) and thinly sliced spring onions
2.5 cm (1") pieces of *daikon* (white radish) and thinly sliced spring onions

1. *Put the* dashi *in a saucepan and set a sieve over it. Rub the* miso *paste through the sieve with the back of a spoon, adding a little* dashi *to help it through.*

2. *Bring the soup to a simmer over moderate heat, pour the soup into individual bowls, and top with the garnish of your choice.*

JAPANESE

Hamaguri Ushiojitate
(Clear Clam Soup with Mushrooms)

(serves 6)

	total	1 of 6 portions
kcal	106	18
fat (g)	2	.3
sodium (mg)	1085	181
dietary fibre (g)	1	.2
cholesterol (mg)	72	12

This soup is an example of the visual artistry of Japanese cooking. It's delicate, faintly lemony and beautifully arranged.

6 C (1.5 L) water
7.5 cm (3") square of *kombu* (dried kelp), rinsed
12 small clams, scrubbed clean
6 small white mushrooms

2 tsp light soyasauce
12 sprigs of watercress, blanched for 1 minute, and cooled
6 paper-thin slices of lime or lemon, seeded

1. *Place water, kombu and clams in a saucepan. Bring to a boil, remove the kombu, and boil 2 minutes, or until the clams open. Skim off any scum. Add mushrooms and soyasauce and boil an additional 30 seconds.*

2. *In each of 6 soup bowls, arrange 2 clams, 2 sprigs of watercress, and a slice of lime or lemon. Pour the hot broth down the side of the bowl to preserve the arrangement and serve immediately.*

JAPANESE

Ichiban Dashi (Basic Stock)

(makes 9 cups or 2.5 litres)

	total
kcal	147
fat (g)	.01
sodium (mg)	25
dietary fibre (g)	.1
cholesterol (mg)	0

This stock provides a fair amount of protein, B vitamins and trace minerals. (Note: nutritional values for this stock are very approximate.)

9 C (2.5 L) water
7.5 cm (3") square of *kombu* (dried kelp),
    rinsed

1 C flaked *katsuobushi* (dried bonito)

1. *Bring water to a boil, drop in the* kombu *and return to the boil, then immediately remove the* kombu *and set aside for* niban dashi *(see next recipe).*

2. *Add the* katsuobushi *to the boiling water, then immediately turn off the heat. Leave the stock to steep for 2 minutes, then strain. Set the* katsuobushi *aside for* niban dashi. Ichiban dashi *will keep in the refrigerator 2 days, or at room temperature for 6-8 hours.*

JAPANESE

Niban Dashi (Vegetable Cooking Stock)

(makes 5 cups or 1.25 litres)

	total
kcal	183
fat (g)	.01
sodium (mg)	25
dietary fibre (g)	.1
cholesterol (mg)	0

(Note: nutritional values for this stock are very approximate.)

kombu (kelp) and *katsuobushi* (dried bonito)
    left from preparing *ichiban dashi* (see
    above)

5 C (1.25 L) water
¼ C additional flaked *katsuobushi*

1. *Put the left-over* kombu *and* katsuobushi *and water in a saucepan. Bring just to the boil, add the additional* katsuobushi, *and reduce the heat to low; simmer 5 minutes.*

2. *Strain the stock, and cool to room temperature.* Niban dashi *will keep 2 days in the refrigerator, or 6-8 hours at room temperature.*

JAPANESE

Shabu Shabu (Beef Steamboat)

(serves 4-6)

	total	1 of 4 portions	1 of 6 portions
kcal	3868	967	645
fat (g)	66	17	11
sodium (mg)	1192	298	199
dietary fibre (g)	51	13	9
cholesterol (mg)	413	103	69

Shabu shabu is a substantial one-pot meal and consequently a little higher in kilocalories and fat than most other recipes. However, it is an excellent source of protein and B vitamins, a good source of vitamin C and beta-carotene, and a fair source of calcium, phosphorus and fibre.

900 g (about 1¾ lb) Chinese cabbage, blanched, drained, cooled and dried
300 g (10 oz) spinach, trimmed, blanched, drained, cooled and dried
700 g (about 1½ lb) tender beef, sliced .3 cm (¼") thick, 10 cm (4") long and 5 cm (2") wide
450 g (15 oz) carrots, cut lengthwise into .6 cm × 5 cm (¼" × 2") strips, blanched, drained, cooled and dried

12 spring onions, cut lengthwise into quarters
300 g (10 oz) Japanese *tofu*, cut into 2.5 cm (1") cubes
16 white mushrooms, trimmed and wiped clean
8 C (2 L) salt-free chicken stock (see recipe page 140)
10 cm (4") square of *kombu* (dried Japanese kelp), rinsed

1. *Place 3 cabbage leaves on top of one another in the centre of a Japanese bamboo sushi mat or a cloth napkin; trim the tough centre stem at the bottom of each leaf; then place 4 spinach leaves down the centre of the cabbage leaves. Now roll the leaves into a tight cylinder, using the mat or napkin, starting at the bottom, and rolling away from you.*

2. *Repeat until all cabbage and spinach is rolled; then cut each cylinder into 2.5 cm (1") lengths.*

3. *Arrange the beef slices, cabbage rolls, carrot strips, spring onions,* tofu *cubes and mushrooms in rows on a large serving platter. (Artistic presentation is half the enjoyment of eating Japanese food). Chill until ready to serve.*

4. *Put the chicken stock into a steamboat with the kombu, bring to a boil, then simmer throughout the meal. Each guest cooks the food of his choice; the broth is served at the end, and the cooked foods are dipped into individual dishes of* Ponzu *and* Goma Joya *dipping sauces (see next recipes).*

Ponzu

	total
kcal	65
fat (g)	1
sodium (mg)	3430
dietary fibre (g)	1
cholesterol (mg)	0

¼ C (65 ml) water
¼ C (65 ml) light soyasauce
¼ C (65 ml) fresh lemon juice
¼ C (65 ml) fresh lime juice

1.   Mix all ingredients and divide among individual sauce dishes.

Goma Joya

	total
kcal	556
fat (g)	42
sodium (mg)	1329
dietary fibre (g)	17
cholesterol (mg)	0

½ C white sesame seeds, toasted and
   pounded to a paste
3 T *sake* (Japanese rice wine)
2 tsp sugar
1½ T light soyasauce
1 T water

1.   Mix all ingredients and divide among individual sauce dishes.

137

Stuffed Squid Soup (Kaeng Chud Pla Muk)

(serves 8-10)

	total	1 of 8 portions	1 of 10 portions
kcal	4045	506	405
fat (g)	35	4	4
sodium (mg)	2392	299	239
dietary fibre (g)	2	.3	.2
cholesterol (mg)	692	87	69

This dish is rich in protein and minerals, especially copper, zinc and iodine. A dark green or deep yellow vegetable and a small serving of brown or white rice makes this a full meal.

1 T coriander stems, minced
1 tsp garlic, minced
¼ tsp salt
¼ tsp freshly ground black pepper
400 g (14 oz) very lean pork, minced
1 tsp fish sauce (*nam pla*)

16 small whole squid, cleaned, eye section of head discarded
10 C (2.5 L) salt-free chicken stock (see recipe page 140)
4 spring onions, cut into 5 cm (2") lengths
fresh basil leaves (substitute: coriander leaves)

1. Combine the coriander stems, garlic, salt, black pepper, pork, and fish sauce, and beat vigorously until the stuffing is smooth and fluffy.

2. Fill each squid body with about 2 T stuffing, put the head back in place, and secure the openings with toothpicks. Form the remaining stuffing into 2.5 cm (1") balls.

3. Bring the stock to a boil in a heavy saucepan; drop in the stuffed squid and the pork balls, and return to the boil, skimming off any foam or scum. Reduce heat to low and simmer uncovered for 10 minutes. Add the spring onions and remove from heat. Serve garnished with fresh basil leaves.

THAI

Thom Yam Soup

(serves 6-8)

	total	1 of 6 portions	1 of 8 portions
kcal	596	99	75
fat (g)	5	.8	.6
sodium (mg)	1854	309	232
dietary fibre (g)	31	5	4
cholesterol (mg)	900	150	113

This low-kilocalorie, low-fat version of a popular favourite is rich in protein, iodine, zinc and copper.

8 C (2 L) water
1 T fish sauce (*nam pla*)
2 T tamarind (*assam*) mixed with 4 T water and strained
3 stems lemon grass (*serai*), crushed
2 fragrant lime leaves
2 tsp sugar
¼ C (65 ml) fresh lime juice

4 bird chillies (*chilli padi*), halved
4 red chillies, seeded and cut into narrow strips
450 g (about 1 lb) prawns, shelled with tail section left intact
¼ C coriander leaves, chopped
¼ C spring onions, sliced into narrow strips

1. Combine water, fish sauce, tamarind water, lemon grass, lime leaves, sugar, lime juice and bird chillies, and bring to a boil. Reduce heat and simmer 10 minutes.

2. Add the red chillies and prawns, and simmer 4-5 minutes. Stir in the coriander and spring onions, and serve.

Salt-Free Chicken Stock

(yields 9-10 cups or 2.5 litres)

Western version:

	total
kcal	200
fat (g)	2
sodium (mg)	208
dietary fibre (g)	0
cholesterol (mg)	0

Asian version:

	total
kcal	185
fat (g)	2
sodium (mg)	189
dietary fibre (g)	0
cholesterol (mg)	0

Note: nutritional values in the charts are very approximate.

1 kg (2.2 lb) chicken, skinned, all visible fat removed, and cut into 10 pieces

10 C (2.5 L) water

For Western recipes:

1 small onion stuck with 2 whole cloves
pinch thyme
1 bay leaf
pinch rosemary
1 large carrot, cut into 4 pieces
1 sprig parsley

For Asian recipes:

1.25 cm (½") piece fresh ginger, smashed
1 clove garlic, smashed
2 spring onions, cut into 4 pieces
1 screwpine (*pandan*) leaf

1. *Put chicken, water and either Western or Asian seasonings in a large pot with a lid. Bring to a boil over moderate heat, reduce heat to very low, partially cover the pan, and simmer for 2 hours. Check that water doesn't boil away; you want to end with 10 C (2.5 L) of stock.*

2. *At the end of the cooking time, press down on the chicken and vegetables to extract any remaining juices; strain the stock, discard the chicken and vegetables (which will have lost their flavour), and cool thoroughly. After cooling, all the fats will have solidified on the surface of the stock — skim and discard all traces. Put stock into easy-storage containers. (It is a good idea to keep a cup or so in the refrigerator, ready to use, and store the rest in the freezer.)*

INTERNATIONAL

Hearty Minestrone Soup

(serves 8-10)

	total	1 of 8 portions	1 of 10 portions
kcal	3812	477	381
fat (g)	41	5	4
sodium (mg)	2450	306	245
dietary fibre (g)	63	8	6
cholesterol (mg)	0	0	0

This Italian home-style favourite is rich in dietary fibre, carbohydrate, and beta-carotene, and a fair source of vitamin C and protein. Grate a little *parmesan* cheese on top, and serve with a wholegrain bread and a fresh vegetable salad to improve the protein and vitamin C values.

3 T polyunsaturated, soft, tub-type margarine
1 C green peas
1 C zucchini, diced
1 C carrots, diced
1 C potatoes, diced
⅓ C celery, thinly sliced
50 g (2 oz) onion, minced
4 cloves garlic, minced
½ C leeks, finely sliced
2 C imported, tinned, Italian tomatoes, drained and coarsely chopped
8 C (2 L) salt-free chicken stock (see recipe page 140)

1 bay leaf
2 parsley sprigs
1 tsp salt
freshly ground black pepper
½ C rice (brown is preferable)
1 C cooked white beans
1 T fresh basil, finely cut (substitute: 1 tsp dried)
½ tsp dried oregano
¼ tsp dried thyme
minced parsley, minced garlic and grated *parmesan* cheese to garnish.

1. *In a large saucepan, melt the margarine over moderate heat. Add the peas, zucchini, carrots, potatoes and celery. Cook for 3 minutes, then add the onion, garlic and leeks and cook until vegetables are soft and lightly browned.*

2. *Stir in the tomatoes, stock, bay leaf, parsley, salt and pepper to taste. Bring to a boil and simmer 25 minutes, partially covered. Then remove bay leaf and parsley, and add the rice, white beans, basil, oregano and thyme. Simmer 20 minutes more, and serve. Garnish at table.*

Mussel Soup

(serves 4-6)

	total	1 of 4 portions	1 of 6 portions
kcal	750	188	125
fat (g)	48	12	8
sodium (mg)	487	122	81
dietary fibre (g)	75	19	13
cholesterol (mg)	200	50	33

This soup — low in kilocalories and a good source of iodine, zinc, protein, vitamin C and vitamin A — makes an excellent low-fat, low-kilocalorie meal when accompanied by wholegrain bread and a fresh salad. (Don't worry about the small amount of liquid called for in the recipe — the mussels produce their own liquid when cooked.)

100 g (4 oz or about 1) onion, minced
¼ C celery, minced
1 tsp garlic, minced
3 T olive oil (extra virgin is preferable)
1 T fresh basil, minced (substitute: 1 tsp dried basil)

freshly ground black pepper to taste
½ C (125 ml) dry white wine
2 C imported, tinned, Italian plum tomatoes, coarsely chopped but not drained
48 small mussels in the shell, well-scrubbed
2 tsp lemon peel, finely grated

1. Mince together the onion, celery and garlic. Heat the olive oil in a saucepan over moderate heat; add the onion, celery and garlic and cook along with the basil and black pepper for 8-10 minutes, until lightly coloured.

2. Add the wine, and boil briskly until it is reduced by half. Then add the tomatoes and their liquid, and simmer uncovered over very low heat for 20 minutes. Add the mussels, cover the pan, and cook over high heat, shaking the pan occasionally so the mussels cook evenly.

3. After 10 minutes, all the mussels should be open; if not, cook 1 minute more, and discard any that are still closed. Garnish with lemon peel and serve in deep soup bowls. (Bring an extra bowl to the table for the empty shells).

INTERNATIONAL

Clam and Tomato Soup

(serves 4-6)

	total	1 of 4 portions	1 of 6 portions
kcal	809	202	135
fat (g)	42	11	7
sodium (mg)	782	196	130
dietary fibre (g)	15	4	3
cholesterol (mg)	144	36	24

This Italian soup is actually hearty enough to be called a stew. It's rich in iodine, protein and zinc, and a good source of vitamin C and beta-carotene. With a loaf of crusty wholegrain bread, a fresh vegetable salad and fresh fruit, you have a light but satisfying meal.

2½ T olive oil (extra virgin is preferable)
1 tsp garlic, minced
½ C (125 ml) dry white wine
4 C imported, tinned, Italian plum tomatoes, drained, squeezed of excess liquid, and coarsely chopped

24 small hard-shell clams in the shell, well-scrubbed
1 C (250 ml) boiling water
4 T parsley, minced

1. In a large saucepan with a lid, heat the olive oil over moderate heat. Add the garlic, and stir for about 30 seconds. Add the wine and tomatoes, and bring to a boil. Then reduce heat, and simmer, partially covered, for 10 minutes.

2. Meantime, drop the scrubbed clams into the boiling water in a heavy 30 cm (12") skillet; cover tightly and steam for 5-8 minutes, or until they open. (Discard any clams that do not open after 8 minutes.) Transfer the clams with tongs to 4-6 soup bowls.

3. Strain all the clam broth remaining in the skillet into the simmering tomato sauce, cook for 2 minutes, and pour over the clams. Sprinkle with minced parsley.

INTERNATIONAL

Carrot Soup

(serves 10-12)

	total	1 of 10 portions	1 of 12 portions
kcal	1345	135	112
fat (g)	5	.5	.4
sodium (mg)	1483	148	124
dietary fibre (g)	35	4	3
cholesterol (mg)	29	3	2

This naturally sweet, colourful, smooth soup is low in kilocalories and fat, rich in beta-carotene and protein, and a fair source of dietary fibre.

1 kg (2.2 lb) carrots, scraped, trimmed and cut into thin slices
1 large leek, trimmed, washed and thinly sliced
1½ C (375 ml) salt-free chicken stock stock (see recipe page 140)

5-6 C (1.25 L – 1.5 L) skim-milk
½ tsp freshly ground black pepper
⅛ tsp freshly grated (or powdered) nutmeg
whole mint leaves, washed
6 spring onions, sliced into fine rings

1. Drop carrots and leek into boiling chicken stock in a large saucepan, reduce heat, cover, and simmer 15 minutes, until carrots are tender. Puree the vegetables with the broth in a blender, food mill or food processor. Carrots should be absolutely smooth.

2. Return pureed carrots and stock to saucepan, and begin adding milk until the soup is creamy, smooth, and thick — the texture of heavy cream. Add pepper and nutmeg. Heat over very low heat, until warmed through, and serve garnished with whole mint leaves and spring onions.

INTERNATIONAL

Egg and Lemon Soup

(serves 6-8)

	total	1 of 6 portions	1 of 8 portions
kcal	2069	345	259
fat (g)	18	3	2
sodium (mg)	214	36	27
dietary fibre (g)	2	.3	.3
cholesterol (mg)	675	113	84

This Greek soup is rich, creamy and spiked with the tang of lemon. It's rich in protein, vitamins B2 and B12, biotin, folic acid and choline, and a good source of iron. (The combination of egg and lemon is one of the simplest thickeners.)

6 C (1.5 L) salt-free chicken stock (see recipe
  page 140)
⅓ C uncooked rice

3 eggs
3 T fresh lemon juice
2 T fresh mint leaves, minced

1. *Bring chicken stock to a boil; pour in rice, reduce heat and simmer for 15 minutes, until the rice is tender but not overcooked.*

2. *Beat the eggs with a whisk or rotary beater until frothy; beat in the lemon juice and stir in ¼ C (65 ml) simmering chicken broth. Then slowly pour the mixture into the simmering chicken broth, stirring constantly. Cook over very low heat 3-5 minutes, until the soup thickens lightly. Do not let the soup boil or it will curdle. Serve garnished with mint leaves and add salt at table if necessary.*

INTERNATIONAL

Cold Yoghurt and Cucumber Soup

(serves 4-6)

	total	1 of 4 portions	1 of 6 portions
kcal	343	86	57
fat (g)	11	3	2
sodium (mg)	1373	343	229
dietary fibre (g)	1	.3	.2
cholesterol (mg)	34	9	6

This Turkish soup is very refreshing and very low in kilocalories and fat. It's also a good source of vitamins B2 and B12, protein, calcium and phosphorus, and a fair source of vitamin C.

2 C plain, skim-milk yoghurt
225 g (8 oz or about 1 medium) cucumber,
  peeled, seeded and coarsely grated
2 tsp white vinegar
1 tsp olive oil

2 tsp fresh mint leaves, minced (substitute:
  ½ tsp dried mint)
½ tsp fresh dill leaves, minced (substitute: ¼
  tsp dried dill)
½ tsp salt

1. *Stir the yoghurt until it is completely smooth. Beat in the grated cucumber, vinegar, olive oil, mint, dill and salt. Do not overbeat. Refrigerate for 2 hours, until completely chilled.*

INDIAN

Mint and Onion Raita

(serves 4-6)

	total	1 of 4 portions	1 of 6 portions
kcal	194	49	32
fat (g)	3	.8	.5
sodium (mg)	677	169	113
dietary fibre (g)	3	.8	.5
cholesterol (mg)	17	4	3

A *raita* is the best possible accompaniment to a curry because it adds a refreshing coolness to the meal, and quite a lot of good nutrition. This one is a good source of protein, calcium and vitamin C; and like all *raitas*, it's low-kilocalorie and low-fat.

3 T fresh mint, finely cut
3 T onions, finely minced
½ tsp red chilli, minced
¼ tsp salt

¼ tsp ground chilli (cayenne)
1 C plain, skim-milk yoghurt
whole mint leaves for garnish

1. Combine all ingredients and mix well. Chill thoroughly, and garnish with whole mint leaves.

INDIAN

Cucumber and Tomato Raita

(serves 4-6)

	total	1 of 4 portions	1 of 6 portions
kcal	193	48	32
fat (g)	4	1	.7
sodium (mg)	1190	298	198
dietary fibre (g)	3	.8	.5
cholesterol (mg)	17	4	3

This *raita* is rich in vitamin C and beta-carotene, and a fair source of protein and calcium.

1 medium cucumber, peeled, seeded, and
 diced into .6 cm (¼") pieces
1 T onion, minced
½ tsp salt
85 g (3 oz or 1 medium) tomato, diced into
 1.25 cm (½") pieces

1 T coriander leaves, chopped
1 C plain, skim-milk yoghurt
1 tsp ground cumin, dry-toasted in a small
 pan for 30 seconds
whole coriander leaves for garnish

1. *Combine cucumber, onion and salt and mix thoroughly. After standing 5 minutes, squeeze out excess moisture. Add tomato and coriander to mixture and toss thoroughly.*

2. *Mix yoghurt and cumin, and add to the diced vegetables. Chill thoroughly and serve garnished with whole coriander leaves.*

INDIAN

Cabbage and Carrot Salad

(serves 4-6)

	total	1 of 4 portions	1 of 6 portions
kcal	193	48	32
fat (g)	2	.5	.3
sodium (mg)	1116	279	186
dietary fibre (g)	32	8	5
cholesterol (mg)	0	0	0

This salad is an excellent source of vitamin C and beta-carotene, it's quick to prepare and makes a colourful, delicious accompaniment to Indian meals.

300 g (10 oz) white cabbage, finely shredded
150 g (5 oz) carrot, peeled and finely
   shredded

3 red chillies, seeded and finely sliced
juice of 3 limes (*limau kesturi*)
½ tsp salt
1 tsp sugar

1. *Place cabbage, carrots, and chillies in a bowl. Combine lime juice, salt, and sugar and add to shredded ingredients. Toss very well, chill thoroughly and serve.*

Tomato, Onion and Beet Salad

(serves 4-6)

	total	1 of 4 portions	1 of 6 portions
kcal	464	116	77
fat (g)	23	6	4
sodium (mg)	1095	274	183
dietary fibre (g)	15	4	3
cholesterol (mg)	0	0	0

This salad is rich in vitamin C and beta-carotene, and a fair source of fibre. It makes an excellent, cooling side dish to curries.

1 T soya oil
½ T mustard oil
2 T lemon juice
1 T mint leaves, finely chopped
1 T coriander leaves, finely chopped
½ tsp salt

250 g (8 oz or about 2) onions, peeled and cut crosswise into slices
250 g (8 oz) beets, peeled and cut crosswise into slices
180 g (6 oz) tomatoes, peeled and cut crosswise into slices
3 green chillies, seeded and finely sliced

1. *Combine soya and mustard oils, lemon juice, mint, coriander and salt, and whisk until well blended. Scatter the vegetable slices evenly in a serving dish, and sprinkle with dressing. Marinate at room temperature 1 hour, then chill thoroughly before serving.*

Mixed Bean Salad

(serves 4-6)

	total	1 of 4 portions	1 of 6 portions
kcal	3133	783	522
fat (g)	44	11	7
sodium (mg)	1055	264	176
dietary fibre (g)	41	10	7
cholesterol (mg)	0	0	0

This is nutritious enough to make a light luncheon dish, accompanied by brown rice or *chapatis*, or even a supper dish, accompanied by *chapatis* and a *raita*. Rich in protein, iron and dietary fibre, and a good source of B vitamins, the dish improves the longer it sits.

1½ C cooked chick-peas (*channa dhal*)
1½ C cooked red kidney beans
1½ C cooked black-eyed peas
4 cloves garlic, pounded
1 T olive oil
½ C spring onions, finely chopped

3 T coriander, finely chopped
2 green chillies, seeded and minced
½ tsp ground cumin
½ tsp salt
½ tsp ground black pepper
3 T fresh lemon juice

1. Drain freshly cooked beans; if using canned beans, rinse and drain thoroughly to be rid of salt, and omit the ½ tsp salt in this recipe. Combine garlic and olive oil and allow mixture to steep for 5 minutes.

2. Combine the spring onions, coriander, chillies, cumin, salt and pepper; add lemon juice and stir. Add garlic and oil mixture, then beans. Toss well, and chill thoroughly before serving.

INDONESIAN

Javanese Bean Curd and Vegetable Salad (Asinan)
(serves 4-6)

	total	1 of 4 portions	1 of 6 portions
kcal	715	179	119
fat (g)	40	10	7
sodium (mg)	2065	516	344
dietary fibre (g)	43	11	7
cholesterol (mg)	0	0	0

This dish is rich in protein, dietary fibre, calcium and B vitamins, and low in kilo-calories.

Sauce:

¼ C red chillies, seeded and minced
1.25 cm (½") piece ginger, minced
2 cloves garlic, minced
4 T vinegar
2 C (500 ml) cold water
1½ T sugar
1 T fish sauce
¼ tsp salt

Salad:

1 C bean sprouts, steamed for 5 minutes
3 pieces firm soyabean cake (*taukwa*), cut in
   1.25 cm (½") cubes
1 C Chinese cabbage, shredded
1 C white radish, thinly sliced (icicle radishes
   are preferable)
½ C pickled mustard greens, soaked and
   thoroughly rinsed to remove salt
½ C roasted peanuts

1. Grind chillies, ginger and garlic to a paste; add remaining sauce ingredients and blend until smooth.

2. Arrange the vegetables and bean curd on a platter; pour sauce over, sprinkle peanuts and serve.

INDONESIAN

Gado Gado (Vegetable Salad with Peanut Sauce)
(serves 4-6)

	total	1 of 4 portions	1 of 6 portions
kcal	1092	273	182
fat (g)	196	49	33
sodium (mg)	2028	507	338
dietary fibre (g)	51	13	9
cholesterol (mg)	460	115	77

This version has much less fat and fewer kilocalories than the original. It's lighter, less rich, less sweet and less salty, but rich in vitamins C and A, dietary fibre and protein.

Sauce:

1 T soya oil
100 g (4 oz or about 1) onion, minced
2 cloves garlic, minced
30 g (1 oz or about 3) green chillies, seeded and pounded
½ stem lemon grass (*serai*), minced and pounded
1 tsp palm sugar (*gula melaka*)
a shaving of shrimp paste (*belacan*)
3 T chunky peanut butter mixed with ½ C (125 ml) water
1 T tamarind (*assam*) mixed with 2 T water, and strained
1 tsp sweet soyasauce (*kicap manis*)
½ tsp salt
¼ C (65 ml) thin coconut milk, mixed with 2 T evaporated milk and 2 T water

Vegetables:

1 C cabbage, coarsely chopped, dropped into boiling water until softened but still slightly crisp
150 g (5 oz) string beans, stringed, cut in half, and dropped into boiling water until tender
200 g (7 oz) spinach, dropped into boiling water until wilted (about 30 seconds)
1 bunch watercress, (about 140 g or 4 oz), trimmed and dropped into boiling water until wilted (about 30 seconds)
150 g (5 oz) bean sprouts, dropped into boiling water for 1 minute
225 g (8 oz) cucumber, peeled and coarsely sliced
150 g (5 oz) white potatoes, scrubbed but not peeled, boiled and coarsely sliced
2 small eggs, hard-boiled, shelled and quartered
1 piece firm soyabean cake (*taukwa*), diced into 1.25 cm (½") cubes
1 shrimp cracker (*keropok*), broken into large pieces

1. *To make the sauce: heat oil over moderate heat and fry onion and garlic until soft. Pound together with chillies, lemon grass, palm sugar and shrimp paste. Place mixture in a saucepan with peanut butter, tamarind, soyasauce, salt, coconut milk, evaporated milk and water. Blend well and simmer 10 minutes over very low heat.*

2. *Throughly drain and dry all vegetables and arrange in this order: cabbage, beans, spinach, watercress, bean sprouts, cucumber, potatoes, eggs and soyabean cake.*

3. *Pour sauce over, and top with crumbled shrimp cracker.*

MALAY

Acar Timun (Cucumber Pickle)

(serves 4-6)

	total	1 of 4 portions	1 of 6 portions
kcal	804	201	134
fat (g)	61	15	10
sodium (mg)	5993	1498	999
dietary fibre (g)	63	16	11
cholesterol (mg)	0	0	0

High in vitamin C and beta-carotene and a fair source of fibre, Acar Timun makes a beautiful accompaniment to meat and fish dishes served with rice.

450 g (about 1 lb) cucumber, peeled, seeded, and cut into .6 cm × 3.75 cm (¼" × 1½") strips
80 g (3 oz or about 2) carrots, scraped and cut the same as the cucumbers
2 red chillies, shredded
150 g (5 oz) onion, cut into .6 cm (¼") wedges
3 tsp salt
6 dried chillies, soaked to soften, and pounded

4 shallots, peeled and thinly sliced
5 cloves garlic
1.8 cm (¾") piece fresh ginger
1.8 cm (¾") piece fresh turmeric (substitute: 1 tsp dried turmeric)
3 candlenuts (substitute: macadamia nuts)
2 T soya oil
½ tsp white sesame seeds
½ C (125 ml) vinegar
1½ T sugar

1. *Start the day before: put cucumber, carrots, chillies and onion in a colander. Add salt, and let stand 2-3 hours. When softened, rinse away all the salt, and dry thoroughly.*

2. *Pound together: dried chillies, shallots, garlic, ginger, turmeric and candle-nuts; heat oil over moderate heat and add pounded ingredients. Fry for 3-4 minutes over moderate heat, then stir in the sesame seeds. Add vinegar and sugar and bring to a boil; reduce heat to a simmer and cook for 3 minutes more. Then add the vegetables, toss well, and let vegetables steep for 1 day before serving.*

MALAY

Kerabu Timun (Cucumber and Dried Prawn Salad)

(serves 6-8)

	total	1 of 6 portions	1 of 8 portions
kcal	217	36	27
fat (g)	2	.3	.3
sodium (mg)	335	56	42
dietary fibre (g)	21	4	3
cholesterol (mg)	80	13	10

This dish is very low in kilocalories and fat, and a fair source of vitamin C and beta-carotene.

225 g (8 oz or 1 large) cucumber, peeled, seeded, and sliced in pieces .6 cm (¼") thick
8 shallots, finely shredded
juice of 3 limes

1 tsp shrimp paste (*belacan*), toasted and pounded
3 fresh red chillies, seeded and pounded
1 T dried prawns, rinsed and pounded
½ tsp sugar

1. Place cucumber in a bowl and mix in shredded shallots and lime juice; toss well.

2. Pound together shrimp paste and chillies and add to cucumber mixture. Add prawns and sugar and toss well.

JAPANESE

Suzuko Mizore-Ae (Grated Radish and Salmon Roe Salad)

(serves 4-6)

	total	1 of 4 portions	1 of 6 portions
kcal	496	124	83
fat (g)	26	7	4
sodium (mg)	3292	823	549
dietary fibre (g)	10	3	2
cholesterol (mg)	850	213	142

This is a beautiful, delicate salad which goes well with light soups, noodles and grilled dishes. It is low in kilocalories and fat, and a fair source of fibre and vitamin C. (If you use grated carrot instead of salmon roe, it also provides a fair amount of beta-carotene.)

Lohan Chai (Vegetarian Stew), page 126, and Fried Leeks, page 63

Cheng T'ng, page 161

225 g (8 oz) *daikon* (Japanese white radish), peeled and finely shredded
1 T fresh lemon juice

170 g (6 oz) salmon roe (substitute: red caviar)
6 sprigs parsley
6 wedges of lemon

1. *Combine daikon and lemon juice and mix thoroughly. Carefully add the salmon roe or caviar, and divide the mixture among 6 small bowls. On 6 small condiment dishes, place a wedge of lemon and a sprig of parsley.*

Variation: substitute 50 g (2 oz) finely shredded carrot for the salmon roe, and add ¼ tsp salt. This version has a total of 98 kilocalories, less than 1 gram of fat, 583 milligrams of sodium, 12 grams of dietary fibre and no cholesterol.

PHILIPPINE

Bitter Melon and Cucumber Salad (Atsara)
(serves 6)

	total	1 of 6 portions
kcal	98	16
fat (g)	.4	.07
sodium (mg)	1029	172
dietary fibre (g)	21	4
cholesterol (mg)	0	0

This salad is very low in kilocalories and fat, a good source of vitamin C, and a fair source of iron and fibre.

560 g (1¼ lb or about 1 medium) bitter melon (or green, unripe papaya)
225 g (8 oz or 1 medium) cucumber, peeled

½ tsp salt
100 g (4 oz) onion, minced
3 T white vinegar

1. *Cut the bitter melon in half, and scoop out the seeds with a spoon. Do the same to the cucumber. Sprinkle the bitter melon with salt, and allow it to drain in a colander for 15 minutes. Squeeze moisture out with your hands, rinse melon thoroughly to remove salt, and slice the melon into .3 cm (⅛") rounds. Cut the cucumber into .3 cm (⅛") rounds.*

2. *Combine bitter melon, cucumber and onions in a serving bowl. Add the vinegar and toss thoroughly. Chill until ready to serve.*

THAI

Prawn and Squid Salad

(serves 8-10)

	total	1 of 8 portions	1 of 10 portions
kcal	1382	173	138
fat (g)	38	5	4
sodium (mg)	2718	340	272
dietary fibre (g)	17	2	2
cholesterol (mg)	1200	150	120

This salad is low in kilocalories, high in protein, iodine, zinc, copper and iron, and a fair source of vitamin C and beta-carotene.

60 g (2 oz) rice vermicelli, soaked in boiling water for 3 minutes and drained

15 g (½ oz) cloud ear fungus, soaked in boiling water for 30 minutes, washed and drained

400 g (14 oz) medium squid, cleaned, blanched in boiling water for 3 minutes, and cut into .6 cm (¼″) rings

500 g (1 lb) small prawns, blanched in boiling water for 2 minutes, cooled and shelled

3 T local lime juice

3 T vinegar

1 T fish sauce (*nam pla*)

3 tsp sugar

2 tsp fruity olive oil

10 shallots, finely sliced

80 g (3 oz) spring onion, sliced into fine rings

20 g (¾ oz or about 2) red chillies, seeded and shredded

½ C fresh mint leaves

¼ C coriander leaves, coarsely chopped

¼ C Chinese celery leaves

3 fragrant lime leaves, shredded

225 g (8 oz or about 1 medium) cucumber, cut into 5 cm × .6 cm (2″ × ¼″) pieces

1. *Cut vermicelli into short pieces and place in a large bowl. Add the cloud ear fungus, blanched squid and prawns. Toss well. Mix the lime juice, vinegar, fish sauce, sugar, and oil, and pour over the vermicelli mixture. Toss well. Add the remaining ingredients, toss well and serve.*

KOREAN

Vegetable Salad with Prawns and Mustard Sauce (Naengchae)
(serves 4-6)

	total	1 of 4 portions	1 of 6 portions
kcal	480	120	80
fat (g)	21	5	4
sodium (mg)	2312	578	385
dietary fibre (g)	5	1	.8
cholesterol (mg)	435	109	73

This dish is rich in protein, iron, zinc, copper and iodine, and a fair source of vitamins C and A.

30 g (1 oz) cabbage, thinly sliced in 1.25 cm × 5 cm (½" × 2") pieces
¼ tsp salt
60 g (2 oz) cucumber, thinly sliced in 1.25 cm × 5 cm (½" × 2") pieces
30 g (1 oz) carrot, thinly sliced in 1.25 cm × 5 cm (½" × 2") pieces
30 g (1 oz) cooked ham, thinly sliced in 1.25 cm × 5 cm (½" × 2") pieces
100 g (4 oz) Korean crispy pear, thinly sliced in 1.25 cm × 5 cm (½" × 2") pieces

100 g (4 oz) small prawns, boiled until just done and shelled
1 egg, lightly beaten

Sauce:

2 T prepared mustard (Dijon or wholegrain)
2 tsp sugar
1 T vinegar
¼ tsp salt

1. *Mix the cabbage with the ¼ tsp salt; set aside for 10 minutes, then rinse, and squeeze out all excess moisture.*

2. *Mix cabbage, cucumber, carrot, ham, pear and prawns in a serving bowl. Heat a non-stick pan over moderate heat and add the beaten egg, swirling the pan to produce a very thin omelette. When the egg is set, peel off the omelette, and slice into 1.25 cm × 5 cm (½" × 2") pieces.*

3. *Add the egg pieces to the vegetables and prawns. Combine the sauce ingredients and pour over the vegetables. Toss well and serve immediately.*

Crispy Pear Salad (Chomuchim)

(serves 6)

	total	1 of 6 portions
kcal	67	11
fat (g)	.7	.1
sodium (mg)	1027	171
dietary fibre (g)	8	1
cholesterol (mg)	0	0

This salad is cool and refreshing, low in kilocalories and fat, rich in vitamin C, and a fair source of beta-carotene.

30 g (1 oz) carrot, peeled and shredded
60 g (2 oz) white radish, peeled and shredded
250 g (8 oz) ripe Korean crispy pear, peeled and shredded

½ tsp salt
1 T vinegar
1 T sugar

1. *Mix shredded ingredients immediately with salt, vinegar and sugar. (Pear will turn brown otherwise.) Chill and serve with* Bulgogi *(see recipe page 37).*

Yoghurt, Vegetable and Herb Salad

(serves 4-6)

	total	1 of 4 portions	1 of 6 portions
kcal	172	43	29
fat (g)	3	.8	.5
sodium (mg)	707	177	118
dietary fibre (g)	2	.5	.3
cholesterol (mg)	17	4	3

This Iranian salad is smooth, light, refreshing, rich in calcium, protein and B vitamins, and a good source of vitamin C. It's also very low in kilocalories and fat.

225 g (8 oz or 1) cucumber, peeled, cut in half, seeded and finely diced
3 T green capsicum, finely diced
3 T spring onions, finely chopped
2 T fresh tarragon, finely chopped (substitute: 1 T dried)

1 T fresh dill, finely chopped (substitute: 1 tsp dried)
½ tsp fresh lemon or lime juice
¼ tsp salt
1 C plain, skim-milk yoghurt

1. Place the cucumber in a deep bowl; add the green capsicum, spring onions, tarragon, dill, lemon juice and salt. Stir well to combine. Add yoghurt and blend well. Refrigerate at least 1 hour before serving.

INTERNATIONAL

French Potato Salad

(serves 4-6)

---

	total	1 of 4 portions	1 of 6 portions
kcal	456	114	76
fat (g)	23	6	4
sodium (mg)	988	247	165
dietary fibre (g)	4	1	.7
cholesterol (mg)	0	0	0

This salad is quite low in kilocalories and fat, rich in carbohydrate, and a fair source of protein, vitamin C and vitamin B6.

1.3 kg (about 3 lb) medium, firm potatoes, scrubbed, but not peeled
boiling water to cover potatoes by 5 cm (2")
¼ C (65 ml) salt-free chicken stock (see recipe page 140)
¼ C (65 ml) white wine vinegar
½ tsp salt

1 tsp Dijon or whole-grain mustard (substitute: ½ tsp dry mustard)
1½ T olive oil
¼ C spring onions, finely sliced
3 T fresh parsley, minced
freshly ground black pepper

1. Drop potatoes into briskly boiling water, and cook uncovered, until they are just done. Drain, and plunge them into cold water for 1 minute. When slightly cooled, slice potatoes into slices .6 cm (¼") thick. (Potatoes must be warm in order to absorb seasonings). Put potato slices in a large bowl and add chicken stock. Toss gently and let potatoes rest until all the liquid is absorbed.

2. Mix together vinegar, salt and mustard and pour over potatoes. Toss gently and again let potatoes rest to absorb seasoning. Now add oil, spring onions and parsley. Toss to combine, add pepper to taste and serve warm, at room temperature or chilled. The salad is better after it sits.

INTERNATIONAL

Asian Vegetable Salad

(serves 6)

	total	1 of 6 portions
kcal	658	110
fat (g)	45	8
sodium (mg)	904	151
dietary fibre (g)	25	4
cholesterol (mg)	0	0

This salad is rich in vitamin C, dietary fibre and beta-carotene. (Note: the nutritional information does not include values for heart of palm.)

150 g (5 oz) cooked lotus root, sliced .6 cm (¼") thick

150 g (5 oz) cooked bamboo shoots, sliced .6 cm (¼") thick

150 g (5 oz) bean sprouts

150 g (5 oz) heart of palm, sliced .6 cm (¼") thick

100 g (4 oz) water convolvulus (*kangkong*) leaves, blanched

100 g (4 oz) watercress, trimmed and blanched

170 g (6 oz or about 2) tomatoes, sliced

120 g (4 oz or about 3) carrots, scraped and finely shredded

Dressing:

1 tsp ginger, finely shredded

3 T soya oil

2 tsp light soyasauce

3 tsp fresh lime juice

3 T water

1. *Arrange all vegetables in circles, lines or piles on a large platter. Steep the ginger in the oil for 15 minutes, then add soyasauce, lime juice and water. Serve dressing separately.*

Sweets

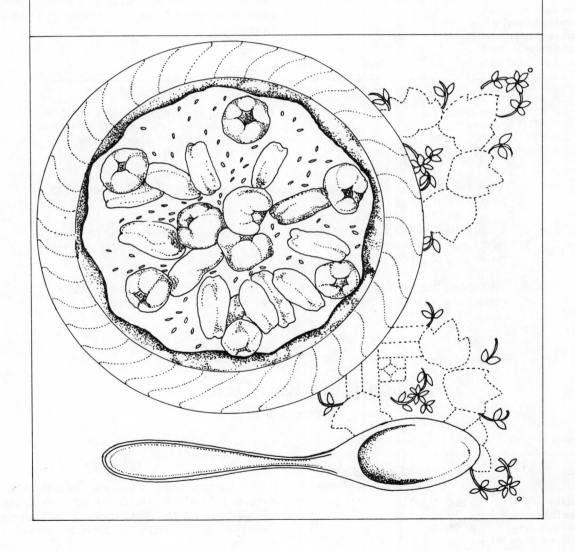

Snow Fungus with Orange Fruit

(serves 4-6)

	total	1 of 4 portions	1 of 6 portions
kcal	413	103	69
fat (g)	1	.3	.2
sodium (mg)	18	4	3
dietary fibre (g)	7	2	1
cholesterol (mg)	0	0	0

This delightful, lightly sweet soup is made with less than half the sugar of the usual recipe. It is a good source of calcium, phosphorus, vitamin C, beta-carotene and dietary fibre.

50 g (2 oz) snow fungus
6 C (1.5 L) water
50 g (2 oz) rock sugar
3 screwpine (*pandan*) leaves

400 g (14 oz) ripe loquats, apricots, mangoes, or peaches, pitted and sliced (Note: if using tinned fruit, be sure to select the kind packed in juice, not heavy syrup)

1. Soak snow fungus in warm water to cover, until completely soft. Remove all foreign matter and drain.

2. Combine snow fungus, water, sugar and screwpine leaves, and bring to a boil. Reduce heat and simmer for 40 minutes uncovered, then cover and simmer an additional 20 minutes over lowest heat.

3. Add sliced fruit, and gently simmer for an additional 5 minutes. Remove from heat, remove screwpine leaves, and serve either hot or chilled.

Longan and Red Date Soup

(serves 4-6)

	total	1 of 4 portions	1 of 6 portions
kcal	960	240	160
fat (g)	7	2	1
sodium (mg)	25	6	4
dietary fibre (g)	29	7	5
cholesterol (mg)	0	0	0

This soup has a lovely contrast of colour and texture. It is a fair source of vitamin C, iron and fibre, but also a bit higher in kilocalories than the other soups, so a small portion is sufficient.

150 g (5 oz) longan meat
40 red dates

6 C (1.5 L) water
75 g (2½ oz) rock sugar

1. *Rinse longan meat and red dates. Put all ingredients into a saucepan and bring to a boil. Reduce heat and simmer for one hour. Serve hot.*

CHINESE

Cheng T'ng

(serves 4-6)

	total	1 of 4 portions	1 of 6 portions
kcal	1809	452	302
fat (g)	4	1	.7
sodium (mg)	80	20	13
dietary fibre (g)	15	4	3
cholesterol (mg)	0	0	0

This dessert is a fair source of protein, fibre, iron, vitamin B1, niacin and biotin.

30 g (1 oz) lotus seeds
120 g (4 oz) ginko nuts
8 C (2 L) water
30 g (1 oz) *pak hup* (available at Chinese medicine shops)

30 g (1 oz) dried longan
60 g (2 oz) dried persimmon
60 g (2 oz) pearl barley
300 g (10 oz) rock sugar
crushed ice

1. *Soak lotus seeds for 15 minutes, split and remove green core. Blanch, skin and split the ginko nuts, and remove bitter core.*

2. *Boil water; add lotus seeds, ginko nuts,* pak hup, *longan and persimmon. Cook over moderate heat until ingredients are soft. Add pearl barley and sugar, and simmer gently until barley is soft. Cool at room temperature and chill in the refrigerator. Serve with crushed ice.*

INTERNATIONAL

Wholewheat Banana Cake

(yields about 18 slices)

	total	1 slice
kcal	2441	136
fat (g)	107	6
sodium (mg)	2318	129
dietary fibre (g)	27	2
cholesterol (mg)	459	26

This cake is much more than just another tasty dessert. It is rich in carbohydrate, dietary fibre and protein, a fair souce of calcium, phosphorus, vitamin B1, niacin, biotin and iron, and quite low in kilocalories and fat.

1 C wholewheat flour
½ C plain, all-purpose flour
⅓ C brown sugar
½ C skim-milk powder
2¼ tsp baking powder
½ tsp nutmeg
½ tsp cinnamon
¼ tsp salt
¼ C walnuts, chopped
¼ C sunflower seeds, chopped (available at health food stores)

¼ C golden raisins
2 eggs
1 C (about 3) bananas, mashed
¼ C polyunsaturated, soft, tub-type margarine, melted
¼ C (65 ml) water
1 tsp vanilla extract
1 23 cm × 12 cm × 7 cm (9" × 5" × 3") loaf pan, greased and floured

1. *Preheat oven to 175°C (350°F or Gas Regulo 6). Combine dry ingredients: wholewheat and plain flours, brown sugar, skim- milk powder, baking powder, nutmeg, cinnamon and salt. Add nuts, seeds and raisins.*

2. *Combine wet ingredients: beat eggs until frothy, then beat in bananas, margarine, water and vanilla. Add wet ingredients to dry, stirring just long enough to thoroughly moisten. Pour batter into prepared pan.*

3. *Bake in the centre of the oven for 40-55 minutes, (tent loosely with tinfoil about 10-15 minutes into the bake to prevent burning), or until a bamboo skewer or cake tester inserted in the centre comes out clean. Cool in the pan 15 minutes, then turn out to cool completely on a wire rack. Let the cake rest overnight to make slicing easier.*

Wholewheat Apple Cake

(yields about 18 slices)

	total	1 slice
kcal	2375	132
fat (g)	98	5
sodium (mg)	1345	75
dietary fibre (g)	18	1
cholesterol (mg)	451	25

This is another cake you can give to children — it is rich in carbohydrate, protein, thiamine, niacin, biotin, vitamins B2 and B12, folacin and choline, and quite low in kilocalories and fat.

½ C brown sugar
1 C wholewheat flour
1 C plain, all-purpose flour
½ tsp baking soda
2 tsp baking powder
2 tsp ground cinnamon
½ tsp ground allspice
½ tsp ground cloves
2 eggs

¼ C polyunsaturated, soft, tub-type margarine, melted and cooled
2 T skim-milk
1½ C ripe, sweet apples, washed, cored but unpeeled, and finely chopped
1 tsp vanilla extract
½ C pumpkin seeds, chopped (available at health food stores)
1 23 cm × 12 cm × 7 cm (9″ × 5″ × 3″) loaf pan, greased

1. *Preheat oven to 175°C (350°F or Gas Regulo 6). Combine dry ingredients: brown sugar, wholewheat flour, plain flour, baking soda, baking powder, cinnamon, allspice and cloves. Blend thoroughly.*

2. *Combine wet ingredients: beat eggs until frothy; add melted margarine, milk, apples and vanilla extract. Add wet ingredients to dry, stirring just long enough to thoroughly moisten dry ingredients; do not overmix. Stir in pumpkin seeds, and pour batter into prepared pan. Bake 45-55 minutes, (tenting the cake loosely with tinfoil about 15 minutes into the bake to prevent burning), or until a bamboo skewer or cake tester inserted into the centre comes out clean.*

INTERNATIONAL

Carrot Cake

(yields about 36 slices from 2 cakes)

	total	1 slice
kcal	3099	86
fat (g)	119	3
sodium (mg)	2269	63
dietary fibre (g)	43	1
cholesterol (mg)	0	0

This is a marvelously rich, moist cake, and it's low in kilocalories and fat, rich in beta-carotene, carbohydrate, dietary fibre, thiamine, and niacin, and a fair source of protein, iron and calcium.

¾ C brown sugar
1¼ C (315 ml) water
3 C (about 4) carrots, finely grated
1 T polyunsaturated, soft, tub-type
  margarine
1 tsp ground cloves
1 tsp ground cinnamon
½ tsp ground allspice
½ tsp ground nutmeg

½ C pumpkin seeds, chopped
½ C sunflower seeds, chopped
1¼ C wholewheat flour
1 C plain, all-purpose flour
2 tsp baking powder
1 tsp baking soda
¼ tsp salt
2 23 cm × 12 cm × 7 cm (9" × 5" × 3") loaf
  pans, lightly oiled

1. *Start the day before. Combine brown sugar, water, carrots, margarine, cloves, cinnamon, allspice and nutmeg in a saucepan. Bring to a boil over high heat, reduce heat to low, and simmer 5 minutes. Turn off the heat, cover, and set aside for 12 hours or overnight.*

2. *Preheat oven to 135°C (275°F or Gas Regulo 3). Combine seeds, wholewheat and plain flours, baking powder, baking soda and salt. Fold dry ingredients into the carrot mixture (after it has rested at least 12 hours), stirring just long enough to combine ingredients.*

3. *Divide batter between the two oiled pans, and bake for 70 minutes, (tenting loosely with tinfoil about 10-15 minutes into the bake to prevent burning), or until the cake tests done when a bamboo skewer or a cake tester inserted in its centre comes out clean.*

INTERNATIONAL

Oatmeal, Orange and Date Bars

(yields 16-20 bars)

	total	1 bar
kcal	3733	187
fat (g)	173	9
sodium (mg)	673	34
dietary fibre (g)	58	3
cholesterol (mg)	225	11

These bars are lower in kilocalories and fat (although they're not low-kilocalorie and low-fat), high in carbohydrate, dietary fibre, vitamin B1 and niacin, and a fair source of protein.

½ C (125 ml) soya oil
1 egg, lightly beaten
1 tsp vanilla extract
1½ tsp orange rind, grated
1¼ C dates, finely chopped
1 C rolled oats
1 C wholewheat flour

1 tsp baking powder
1 tsp ground cinnamon
½ tsp ground allspice
½ C sunflower seeds
⅔ C (170 ml) orange juice
1 32 cm × 23 cm (13" × 9") baking pan,
   lightly oiled

1. Preheat oven to 175°C (350°F or Gas Regulo 6). Combine the wet ingredients: oil, egg, vanilla, orange rind, and dates. Mix well.

2. Combine the dry ingredients: oats, flour, baking powder, cinnamon, allspice and sunflower seeds. Blend thoroughly, then add to the wet ingredients. Stir in the orange juice.

3. Spread the mixture evenly in the oiled baking pan; bake 20-25 minutes, cool 3 minutes in the pan, and cut into 16-20 bars.

Gula Melaka and Peanut Butter Biscuits

(yields 36 biscuits)

	total	1 biscuit
kcal	1924	53
fat (g)	96	3
sodium (mg)	4485	125
dietary fibre (g)	13	.4
cholesterol (mg)	225	6

These cake-like biscuits are delicate, moist and filled with peanut butter flavour. They're lower in fat and kilocalories than regular biscuits (although they're not low-kilocalorie and low-fat), high in carbohydrate, a good source of protein, vitamins B1 and B2, niacin, biotin and dietary fibre, and a fair source of iron.

½ C palm sugar (*gula melaka*, or substitute: brown sugar)
⅓ C polyunsaturated, soft, tub-type margarine
½ C peanut butter, smooth or chunky, as preferred
1 egg
1 tsp vanilla

¾ C wholewheat flour
½ C plain, all-purpose flour
¾ tsp baking soda
½ tsp ground or freshly grated nutmeg
2 T raw white sesame seeds
1 egg white, lightly beaten in 1 tsp water
½ C plain, unsweetened wheat germ
lightly greased baking sheets

1. Preheat oven to 175°C (350°F or Gas Regulo 6). Beat the palm sugar, margarine and peanut butter until light and fluffy; then beat in the egg and vanilla.

2. Combine the dry ingredients: thoroughly mix wholewheat and plain flours, baking soda, nutmeg and sesame seeds; fold dry ingredients into peanut butter mixture, stirring only until dry ingredients are thoroughly mixed.

3. Form dough into 2.5 cm (1") balls; dip in beaten egg white, then roll in wheat germ. Place 3.75 cm (1½") apart on the baking sheets, and bake 8-10 minutes; do not allow to over-brown. Let cool 2 minutes on baking sheets, then remove to wire racks to cool completely.

Oatmeal, Raisin and Carrot Biscuits

(yields 36-48 biscuits)

	total	1 of 36 biscuits	1 of 48 biscuits
kcal	3182	88	66
fat (g)	101	3	2
sodium (mg)	1513	42	32
dietary fibre (g)	35	.9	.7
cholesterol (mg)	236	7	5

These biscuits are fairly low in kilocalories and fat, and high in carbohydrate, protein, iron, dietary fibre, beta-carotene and vitamin B complex.

⅓ C (85 ml) soya oil
¼ C brown sugar
¼ C unsulphured molasses
1 egg, lightly beaten
1 C wholewheat flour
½ tsp baking powder
½ tsp baking soda
¼ tsp nutmeg

¼ C skim-milk powder
¼ tsp salt
1 tsp cinnamon
1 C (about 2) carrots, grated
½ C raisins
1¼ C quick-cooking rolled oats
1 baking sheet, lightly oiled

1. Preheat oven to 205°C (400°F or Gas Regulo 8). Combine oil, brown sugar, molasses and egg. In another bowl, combine flour, baking powder, baking soda, nutmeg, skim-milk powder, salt and cinnamon. Add dry mixture to the oil mixture, and blend only long enough to moisten. Stir in the carrots, raisins and oats, and mix well. Do not overmix.

2. Place a rounded teaspoonful of dough for each biscuit on the baking sheet; space them 5 cm (2") apart. Bake 10 minutes, or until lightly browned around the edges. Cool on wire racks.

Apricot and Oatmeal Biscuits

(yields 36 biscuits)

	total	1 biscuit
kcal	3291	91
fat (g)	153	4
sodium (mg)	597	17
dietary fibre (g)	30	.8
cholesterol (mg)	227	6

These biscuits are a good source of carbohydrate, fibre, thiamine and niacin, and a fair source of protein.

1 C rolled oats
¼ C sunflower seeds, chopped
½ C wholewheat flour
½ C plain, all-purpose flour
1 tsp baking powder
½ tsp cinnamon
⅛ tsp nutmeg

¼ C (65 ml) soya oil
⅓ C (85 ml) honey
1 egg, lightly beaten
½ C (125 ml) skim-milk
1 tsp vanilla extract
½ C dried apricots, finely chopped
1 baking sheet, lightly oiled

1. *Start the night or morning before: combine oats, sunflower seeds, flours, baking powder, cinnamon and nutmeg; blend well.*

2. *Combine oil, honey, egg, milk and vanilla. Add to the dry ingredients, and stir until moistened. Stir in the apricots, and refrigerate, covered with plastic wrap, for at least 4 hours, preferably overnight.*

3. *Preheat oven to 175°C (350°F or Gas Regulo 6). Place a rounded teaspoonful of dough for each biscuit on the baking sheet, leaving 5 cm (2") between each. Bake 12 minutes, or until a light, golden brown. Remove to racks to cool.*

Steamed Fish with Black Beans and Chilli, page 44

Acar Fish (Pickled Fish), page 50, and Nasi Kunyit (Turmeric Rice), page 94

References

Bright-See, Elizabeth and Gail McKeown-Eyssen. "Estimation of per capita crude and dietary fibre supply in 38 countries," American Journal of Clinical Nutrition, 1984, 39: 821-829.

"Food Composition Table for Use in East Asia." United States Department of Health, Education and Welfare, Nutrition Program Center for Disease Control, Health Services and Mental Health Administration, and Food and Agriculture Organization of the United Nations, Food Policy and Nutrition Division, December 1972, reprinted in 1978, DHEW Publication No: (NIH) 79-465.

Gopalan, C., B.V. Rama Sastri and S.C. Balasubramanian. *Nutritive Value of Indian Foods*, National Institute of Nutrition, Indian Council of Medical Research, Hyderabad, India, 1980.

"Nutrient Composition of Malaysian Foods — A Preliminary Table." Compiled by Tee E. Siong, Division of Human Nutrition, Institute for Medical Research, Kuala Lumpur, Malaysia, 1982.

Paul, A.A. and D.A.T. Southgate. *McCance and Widdowson's — The Composition of Foods*, 4th revised and extended edition of MRC Special Report No. 297, London, Her Majesty's Stationery Office, Amsterdam, New York, Oxford, Elsevier/North Holland Biomedical Press, 1978.

Robinson, C.H. *Fundamentals of Normal Nutrition*, 3rd edition, Macmillan Publishing Company, New York, 1978.

English, Chinese and Malay Names of Asian Foods

English Name	Chinese Name	Malay Name
Cereal and Grain Products		
Barley,		Barli
whole grain	大麦	
pearled, light	薏米	beras barli
Maize, corn,	玉蜀黍	Jagung
flakes	玉蜀黍片	emping jagung
starch	蜀米粉	tepung jagung
Oats,	燕麦	Oat
oatmeal/rolled oats	麦片	tepung oat/emping oat
Rice,	米	Beras
brown/hulled	糙米	beras kampong
undermilled/homepounded	糙米	
milled, polished	白米	beras kilang
parboiled	占米	beras keling
flour	占米粉	tepung beras
cooked, milled		̫
, undermilled		
noodles, freshly made	果条	keow teow
, dried	米粉	mi hoon
Rice, glutinous,	糯米	Pulut
brown/hulled	麦米	
milled	白糯米	pulut putih
flour	糯米粉	tepung pulut
Rice, black	黑糯米	Pulut hitam
glutinous		
Wheat,	小麦	Gandum
flour, white wheat	面粉	tepung gandum
biscuits, plain	饼干	biskut ringkas
macaroni; spaghetti	通心粉	macaroni; spageti
noodles, dried	面干	mi kuning
, instant	快熟面	mi semerta/segera
breads,	面包	roti
, wholemeal	全麦面包	roti gandum tulin
, white	白面包	roti putih
cake, sponge	蛋糕	kek span

Starchy Roots, Tubers and Fruits

Arrowroot starch	葛根粉糊	Tepung ubi garut
Cassava, bitter,	木薯	Ubi kayu
root,	木薯根	akar
flour/meal	木薯粉	tepung
starch	木薯粉糊	kanji
Plantain, cooking banana, raw	热带蕉	Pisang tandok
Potato, white:	马铃薯	Ubi kentang
tuber, raw		
, boiled		kentang, rebus
chips, fried	油炸薯片	kentang, goreng
Sagopalm noodles	冬粉	Mi sagu
Sweetpotato, tuber	蕃薯	Keledek
raw, pale variety		
, yellow variety		
boiled, yellow		
Taro, dasheen	芋	Talas, keladi
tuber, raw		
, boiled		
Yam, Chinese; Spiny yam	芋头	Ubi keladi
tuber, raw		

Grain Legumes and Legume Products

Broadbean; horsebean	扁豆	Kacang buncis besar
whole seeds, dried		
fried and salted		
Chickpea; Bengal gram	鸡仔豆	Kacang cick
whole seeds, dried		
Green gram; red bean, Mung bean	绿豆；红豆	Kacang merah; Kacang hijau
whole seeds, dried		
powdered, instant;		
sugar and flour added, green bean		
Lentil; dhal; split pea	印度扁豆	Kacang dal
whole seeds, dried		
Mung bean, black gram	黑豆	Kacang cendai
whole seeds, dried		
Peanut; groundnut	花生	Kacang tanah
raw		
boiled		
dried		
roasted, with shell		
roasted, without shell		
roasted, salted		
peanut butter, salt added	花生酱	
Peas, garden or field	菁豆	Kacang pis

English Name	Chinese Name	Malay Name
Peas: dried		
parched, salted		
Soyabean, yellow	黄豆	Kacang soya
seeds, dried		
Soyabean, whole seeds		
salted, black	豆豉	tau cheow
, fermented	豆酱	
Soyabean products:		
curd, unpressed	水豆腐	
curd, tofu	水豆腐	
raw, plain		
dried, spongy square	豆腐包	
Soyabean products:		
curd, tofu dried, rope-like	腐竹干	tahu kering
commercial (fermented with chilli pepper)	腐乳	
Curdsheet, dried type	甜腐竹干	
Curdcake, pressed raw, plain	豆干	
Soyabean milk	豆奶	air tahu
Soyabean sauce	酱油	kicap
dark, thick	黑酱油	
light, thin	酱青	
Tempeh	发酵黄豆	tempeh
Nuts and Seeds		
Almond	杏仁	Badam
unblanched, dried		
roasted and salted		
Candlenut seeds	毛卡拉	Buah keras
dried		
Cashewnuts	腰豆	Biji gajus/biji janggus
dried		
roasted with oil		
Chestnut, Chinese	栗果	Buah berangan
raw		
roasted		
Coconut	椰子	Buah kelapa
mature, raw		
Cream	浓椰浆	Santan
prepared without water	椰浆	peti santan
prepared with water	稀椰浆	
Milk	椰浆	
Water	椰水	air kelapa
Ginkgo seeds	白果	
whole seeds, dried		

Lotus seeds	蓮子	Biji teratai
dried		
Pumpkin seeds	南瓜子	Kua ci
dried and salted		
Sesame, oriental	芝麻	Biji bijan
seeds, black or white		
Sunflower seeds	向日葵子	Biji bunga matahari
dried		
Watermelon seeds	西瓜子	Biji melikai/temikai
dried		
Vegetables and Vegetable Products		
Amaranth, Chinese spinach	波菜	Bayam
leaves and stems, raw		
Amaranth, sp.	莧菜	Bayam
leaves and stems, green		
red		
white		
Bamboo shoots	竹筍	Rebung
raw		
canned		
Beans, snap or string	龟豆／菜豆	Kacang buncis/Kacang panjang
green variety		
Bittergourd, Balsam pear	苦瓜	Peria/Kambas
fruit, raw		
Brinjal, egg-plant aubergine		Terung
raw, purple and white varieties		
Cabbage		Kubis
pekinese, raw	黄芽白菜	kubis cina
pai-tsai, raw	本地白菜	
headed (white variety), raw	包心菜	
Carrot	胡萝卜	Lobak merah
raw		
Cassava, bitter	木薯叶	Ubi kayu
leaves, raw		
Cauliflower	椰菜花	Bunga kubis
raw		
Celery, Chinese	芹菜	Selderi
unbleached, raw		
bleached, raw		
Chives	韭菜	Kucai
raw		
Chrysanthemum, crowndaisy	蓬蒿菜	
leaves, raw		
Cabbage, flowering type, raw		

English Name	Chinese Name	Malay Name
Cabbage: Chye sim	菜心	Sawi
Collard; kale	芥兰	Kailan
raw		
Cucumber	黄瓜	Timun
raw		
pickled		acar timun
hairy, raw	毛瓜	
Drumstick leaves; horseradish		Daun kelur
leaves, raw		
pods, raw		
Garlic bulbs	蒜头	Bawang putih
raw		
Ginger roots	薑	Halia
raw		
Gourd, rag, angle-type	角瓜（丝瓜）	Ketola sanding
raw		
Green gram sprouts	豆芽	Taugih
raw		
Jew's ear; Juda's ear; Woodear	黑木耳	
dried, soaked, drained		
Jew's ear, white	白木耳	
dried		
Kangkong; water convulvolus	蕹菜	Kangkung
leaves and stems, raw		
Leek	韮	Daun bawang kucai
raw, unbleached		
Lady's finger; okra	羊角豆	Kacang bende
raw		
Lettuce, garden	生菜	Daun salad
unheaded, raw	本地生菜	
headed, raw	包心生菜	
Lettuce, prickly, Chinese		
leaves, raw		
stems, raw		
Lotus, Hindu	蓮藕	Teratai
tuber, raw		
Maize, yellow; corn	玉蜀黍	Jagung
cooked		
babycorn (canned)	黍米心	
Matai; water chestnut	马蹄	Ma thai
corms, raw		
Mungkuang; yambean	番葛	Sengkuang
tuber, raw		

Mushroom, Chinese	冬菰	Cendawan Cina
dried		
dried, soaked, drained		
Mushroom, straw	草菰	
raw		
dried, soaked, drained		
canned, drained solids		
Mustard greens	芥菜	Sawi bunga
leaves and stems, raw		
salted		
Onion, common, garden	大葱头	Bawang besar
mature, raw		
Onion, fragrant; Chinese leek	大蒜	
raw		
Papaya	木瓜	Betik
fruit, unripe		
Peas, edible-podded	青豆	
young pods, raw		
Peas, garden	青豆	Kacang pis
canned, drained solids		
Peppers, red; tabasco; Chilli peppers	辣椒	Cili merah
Fruit, raw		
, dried	辣椒干	cili kering
, paste	辣椒酱	sambal
Peppers, sweet	灯笼椒	
fruit, green, raw	青灯笼椒	
fruit, red, raw	红灯笼椒	
Petai; stinkbean	臭豆	Petai
fruit, raw		
Pumpkin	金瓜	Labu lemak
fruit, raw		
Radish, oriental; Japanese or Chinese Daikon	萝卜	Lobak cina
roots, raw		
roots, salted, semi-dried, chopped	菜保	
Seaweeds, common varieties; Agar	燕菜	Agar-agar
dried		
dried, soaked, drained		
Shallot	小葱头	Bawang merah
bulbs, raw		
Soyabean sprouts	大豆芽菜	Taugih kacang soya
raw		
Spinach, Ceylon; Vinespinach; Malabar nightshade		
leaves		
Spring onion; onion, welsh	青葱	Daun bawang

English Name	Chinese Name	Malay Name
Spring Onion: raw		
Sweetpotato	蕃薯叶	Keledek
leaves & tender tips, raw		
Tomato	蕃茄	Tomato
ripe, raw		
unripe, raw		
canned		
catsup, bottled	蕃茄酱	kicap tomato
juice, canned	茄汁	air tomato
Turnips	芜菁	Turnip
roots, raw		
Watercress	西洋菜	Selada air
leaves and stems, raw		
Waxgourd, Chinese; ashgourd; winter melon	冬瓜	Kundor
raw		
Fruits		
Apple, common	苹果	Buah epal
fruit, raw		
Banana, common	香蕉	Pisang
fruit, raw, ripe		
Bilimbi	酸杨桃	Bilimbing buluh
fruit, raw		
Chiku; Sapodilla	仁心果	Ciku
fruit, raw		
Custardapple; bullocksheart	蕃荔枝	Buah nona
fruit, raw		
Date:	枣	Kurma/tamar
fruit, preserved Chinese; jujube; common		
fruit, dried		
Indian or Malay	印度枣	
jujube, fruit, raw		
Durian	榴梿	Durian
fruit, raw		
cake	榴梿糕	
Grapes	葡萄	Anggur
raw		
dried (raisins)	葡萄干	
Grapefruit	西洋柚	Limau matakerbau
fruit, raw		
Guava, common	蕃石榴	Jambu batu/biawas
fruit, raw		
Honeydew; Spanish melon; muskmelon	蜜瓜	
raw		

Jackfruit	波罗蜜	Nangka
fruit, mature, raw		
Kedondong; Ambarella	大平洋	Kedondong
fruit, raw	楂椊	
Langsat; domestic duku	黄皮	Langsat, duku
fruit, raw		
Lemon	柠檬	Limau kuning
fruit, raw		
juice, fresh	柠檬汁	
Lime	酸柑	Limau nipis
fruit, raw		
juice, fresh	酸柑汁	
Lychee	荔枝	Lychi
fruit, raw		
, dried with shells	荔枝干	
, canned	罐庄荔枝	
Longan	龙眼	Longan
fruit, raw		
, dried	龙眼干	
, canned	罐庄龙眼	
Malaya roseapple; Ohia	枇杷	Jambu mawar
fruit, raw		
Mango, common; Indian mango	芒果	Mangga
fruit, raw, ripe		
Mango, kuwini	瓜年	Kuwini
fruit, raw		
Mangosteen	山竹	Manggis
fruit, raw		
Mata kuching; cat's eyes	本地龙眼	Mata kucing
fruit, raw		
Olive, Ceylon	橄榄	Buah zaitun
semi-dried, salted	咸橄榄	
sugared	甜橄榄	
Orange, mandarin; tangerine	柑；桔	Limau manis, mandarin/orange tanjerin
fruit, raw		
Orange, sweet	橙	Limau manis
fruit, raw		
juice, fresh	鲜橙汁	
Papaya	木瓜	Betik
fruit, raw		
Passionfruit; granadilla	西番莲果	Buah susu/belewa
juice, fresh (yellow)		
Pear	梨	Pear
fruit, raw		

English Name	Chinese Name	Malay Name
Persimmon, kaki	柿	
fruit, raw, soft-type		
Pineapple	黄梨	Nenas
fruit, raw		
canned		
Plum	李	Plam
fruit, raw		
Pomelo; shaddock	柚	Limau bali;
		Limau abung
		Limau besar
		Limau betawi
		Limau bol
		Buah menteng
fruit, raw		
Rambai		Rambai
fruit, raw		
Rambutan	红毛丹	Rambutan
fruit, raw		
Soursop	番榴连	Durian belanda
fruit, raw		
Starfruit; Carambola	杨桃	Bilimbing besi
fruit, raw		
Sugarcane	甘蔗	Tebu
stalk, peeled, raw		
juice	甘蔗汁	
Waterapple; jambu	水翁	Jambu air
fruit, raw		
Watermelon	西瓜	Melikai, temikai
Fruit, raw		
red pulp variety		
yellow pulp variety		
Sugars and Syrups		
Honey	蜜糖	Madu
Jams, made from		Jem
Apple	苹果酱	
Apricot	杏果酱	
Mango	芒果酱	
Pineapple	黄梨酱	
Strawberry	草每酱	
Jellies (clear jams)	冻子	Lengkong
all kinds		
marmalade, orange		
Molasses	糖浆	Molasses

medium		
Sugar	糖	Gula
crude, brown	黃糖	gula perang
granulated	砂糖	gula pasir
Meat, Poultry and Game		
Bacon, cured		Dendeng-babi
Beef, carcass, fresh	牛肉	Daging lembu
very lean		
medium fat		
fat		
bovril	牛肉汁	
Blood		Darah
chicken, coagulated uncooked	鸡血	
duck, coagulated cooked	鸭血	
Chicken	鸡	Ayam
very young birds, raw		
young birds, raw		
mature birds, raw		
drumstick, raw	鸡腿	peha ayam
wing, raw	鸡翼	kepak
Duck, domesticated	鸭	Itik
meat, raw		
, roasted	烤鸭	
Gizzard		Tembolok
chicken, raw	鸡沙囊	
Goat	山羊	Kambing
meat, raw, lean		
, medium fat		
, fat		
Heart, raw		Jantong
beef	牛心	
chicken	鸡心	
pig	猪心	
Intestines, raw		Tali usus
beef	牛肠	
chicken	鸡肠	
duck	鸭肠	
pig	猪肠	
Kidney, raw		Buah pinggang
beef	牛腰子	
pig	猪腰子	
Liver, raw		Hati
beef	牛肝	
chicken	鸡肝	

English Name	Chinese Name	Malay Name
Liver: duck	鸭肝	
pig	猪肝	
Lung		Paru–paru
beef, raw	牛肺	
pig, raw	猪肺	
Mutton, lamb	绵羊肉	Daging kambing
lean		
medium fat		
Pork		Babi
Carcass, fresh	猪肉	
lean		
medium fat		
feet, fresh	猪脚	
spareribs, fresh lean	猪排骨	
Ham, smoked	火腿	ham
lean		
medium fat		
Pork, roasted	烧肉	
Pork meat, flavoured and soyabean sauce, paste, added	卤猪肉	
Sausage made of:		Sosej
pork, soyabean sauce and spices added (Chinese style)	腊肠	
pork, liver soyabean sauce and spices, added (Chinese style)	腊润肠	
Stomach,		Perut
beef, raw	牛肚	
pig, raw	猪肚	
Tail		Ekor
pig, raw	猪尾	
ox, raw	牛尾	
Tongue		Lidah
beef, raw	牛舌	
pig, raw	猪舌	
Eggs		
Duck egg	鸭蛋	Telur itik
cooked, whole		
salted, raw	咸鸭蛋	telur asin
preserved, limed	皮蛋	telur awitan
Hen egg	鸡蛋	Telur ayam
raw, whole		
, white	鸡蛋白	
, yolk	鸡蛋黄	kuning telur

Quail egg	鹌鹑蛋	Telur burong puyoh
raw, whole		
Fish and Shellfish		
Abalone, canned	罐庄鲍鱼	Abalone
drained solids only		
Anchovy	江鱼仔	Ikan bilis
dried		
boiled and dried		
Ark shell, chestshell	蚶	Kerang
raw		
Clam, razor	蛤（大头）	Kupang
raw		
Crab, sea, blue	蠘	Ketam renjong
raw		
Cuttlefish	鱿鱼	Sotong
raw		
dried	鱿鱼干	sotong kering
Dorab; wolf herring; Silverbar fish	西刀鱼	Parang-parang
raw		
Fish, unclassified		
Large fish, flesh, raw		
high fat		
low fat		
salted, dried		
Small fish, whole		
raw		
dried		
steamed		
Fish roe	鱼卵	Telur ikan
raw		
Goatfish; red mullet	红鱼	
raw		
Grouper, spotted	猴鱼（石斑鱼）	Kerapu
raw		
Hairtail; ribbonfish; cutlass fish	带鱼	Langai Timah, Selayur
raw		
Hardtail; torpedo	硬尾鱼	Cencaru
raw		
Lobster	龙虾	Udang karang
raw		
Mackerel, rake-gilled; striped mackerel	甘蒙鱼	Kembong
raw		
Mackerel, Spanish kingfish	峇冬（马鲛）	Tenggiri batang, Tenggiri papan
raw		

English Name	Chinese Name	Malay Name
Nempterid; ribbon-finned	红哥里	Kerisi
raw		
Octopus, common	八爪鱼	
raw		
Oyster	蚝	Kepah
raw		
dried	蚝干	
Oyster, Sp		Kepah
raw		
Oyster sauce bottled, salt added	瓶庄蚝油	Sos kepah
Pomfret, black	乌鲳	Bawal hitam
raw		
Pomfret, white	白鲳	Bawal putih
raw		
Prawns, marine, shrimp	虾	Udang
raw		
medium		
jumbo		
dried	虾米	udang kering
salted and fermented	今夹洛	cencaluk
paste	虾膏	petis
Sardine, fimbriated	沙丁鱼	Tamban sisek
raw		
Sardine sp; canned	罐庄沙丁鱼	
in oil		
in tomato sauce		
Scad, big-eyed	大目龙	Selar
raw		
Scad, round	吊景	Selayang
raw		
Sea-slug; sea cucumber	海参	Tertipang
dried, edible muscle		
dried, edible muscle, soaked		
Shark sp.	鲨鱼	Yu pasir
raw		Yu nipah
		Yu kepak hitam
Shark Fins	鱼翅	
dried		
dried, soaked, drained		
Snapper, red, Malabar	红鸡	Ikan merah
Sprat; round herring	暹冬	Taman jeboh
raw		

Squid	墨鱼	Sotong
raw		
dried	墨鱼干	
dried, soaked, drained		
Stingray, blue spotted	花点金方	Pari lalat
raw		
Threadfin, four-fingered	午鱼 (马友鱼)	Kurau
raw		
Tilapia		Tilapia
raw		
Milk and Milk Products		
Cheese	乳酪	Kiju
cheddar		
processed		
Ice cream	雪糕	Ice cream.
regular		
rich		
Milk, cow	牛奶	Susu lembu
fluid 3.5% fat		
buttermilk		
dried, imported whole	奶粉	tepong susu
nonfat milk solids (skim), instant	即溶脱脂牛奶	
Canned		
evaporated, unsweetened	浓缩奶水	susu sejat
condensed, sweetened	炼奶	susu pekat
Milk, goat	羊奶	Susu kambing
fluid, whole		
Sherbet		
Yoghurt (skimmed milk)		
Oils and Fats		
Butter, imported	牛油	Mentega
salted	加盐牛油	
Lard	猪油	Lemak babi
Margarine, fortified	面包油	Marjarin
Oils, pure cooking		Minyak masak
Coconut oil	椰油	
Peanut oil	花生油	
Beverages		
Beer	啤酒	Bir
Bovril	牛肉汁	
Carbonated beverages	汽水	
Coconut	椰子	Kelapa
Cream	浓椰浆	santan
prepared without water	椰浆	pati santan

English Name	Chinese Name	Malay Name
Coconut: prepared with water	稀椰浆	
Milk	椰浆	air kelapa
Water	椰水	Air
Juices		
lemon	柠檬汁	Lemon
lime	酸柑汁	Limau nipis
orange, fresh	鲜橙汁	Limau manis
passionfruit, fresh	西番莲汁	Buah susu
sugar cane	甘蔗汁	Tebu
tomato, canned	罐庄蕃茄汁	Tomato
Miscellaneous		
Chocolate	朱古力	Cokelat
sweet		
Salad dressings	沙律油	Kuah salad
Italian		itali
mayonnaise		mayonis
Sauces		Sos
oyster sauce	蚝油	sos kepak
Soyabean sauce	酱油	sos kicap
dark, thick	黑酱油	
light, thin	酱青	
tomato catsup	蕃茄酱	kicap tomato